Date Due

APR 1 8 '96 NOV 2 2 '98 DEC 0 4 2006 OCT 2 8 2008			

The Springer Series
on Death and Suicide

ROBERT KASTENBAUM, Ph.D., Series Editor

Joseph Richman, Ph.D., has been on the faculty of the Albert Einstein College of Medicine in New York City since its founding in 1955, and is now Professor Emeritus. He has also been a Senior Psychologist at the Bronx Municipal Hospital Center, from 1955–1989. He is a faculty member of the New York Center for Psychoanalytic Training, a professional in private practice, and the founder and president of the New York State Association of Suicidology. Dr. Richman is a Fellow of the American Orthopsychiatric Association and of the Society for Personality Assessment. He has been a member of the American Association of Suicidology since its inception in 1968. He also maintains membership in the International Association for Suicide Prevention and Crisis Intervention, the American Group Psychotherapy Association, the American Psychological Association, and the American Gerontological Association, among others.

Dr. Richman received his Ph.D. from Columbia University. He has published over 75 books, articles, and book chapters on gerontology, depression, suicide, and related subjects for the professional public. His book, also published by Springer (1986), *Family Therapy for Suicidal People* is the definitive work in its field. In 1992 he was a co-editor of the comprehensive volume, *Suicide and the Older Adult.*

Over the years Dr. Richman has treated over 800 depressed and/or suicidal persons and their relatives. He has supervised, taught, and served as a consultant to psychiatrists, psychologists, social workers, counselors, nurses, and other members of the mental health professions. In addition, he has conducted seminars and workshops for hospitals, clinics, suicide prevention centers, hot-line counselors, crisis-center volunteers, other gatekeepers, and the lay public. His emphasis is on enhancing life by working with the caring and healing forces of the person in despair, and the family. *Preventing Elderly Suicide* represents the culmination of his life's work, applied to helping the despairing and suicidal adult.

PREVENTING ELDERLY SUICIDE

Overcoming Personal Despair, Professional Neglect, and Social Bias

JOSEPH RICHMAN, PhD

Springer Publishing Company • New York

Copyright © 1993 by Springer Publishing Company

Springer Publishing Company, Inc.
536 Broadway
New York, NY 10012–3955

93 94 95 96 97 / 5 4 3 2 1

Library of Congress Cataloging-in-Publication Data

Preventing elderly suicide : overcoming personal despair, professional
  neglect, and social bias / Joseph Richman.
       p.   cm. — (Springer series on death and suicide ; v. 11)
    Includes bibliographical references and index.
    ISBN 0–8261–7480–9
    1. Aged—Suicidal behavior—Prevention.   I. Series.
RC569.P74   1993
618.97′685844505—dc20   92–35955
                                                                          CIP

Printed in the United States of America

Contents

Introduction

> Time is on the side of therapy work, which really means that time is on the side of life.
>
> —Henry Kellerman (1990)

The purpose of this book is to address why the elderly commit suicide and how we can help them. The reader is introduced to the last stage of life, a period that Erikson (1950) called ego integrity, when we tie it all together and make sense of what has happened to the world and to ourselves.

As Robert Browning said in his poem "Rabbi Ben Ezra," this is the last for which the first was made, when the aged can relax and reap the fruits of a lifetime of labor. They have never before had it so good. Why, then, are the elderly committing suicide in such large numbers? This book addresses that question and its larger implications, not only for psychotherapy but for the basis of a full life in old age. The principles of psychotherapy of a suicidal state are the same as those for successful aging.

Suicide in the elderly is treatable and preventable. This observation is based upon a solid bedrock of research and study, as well as a quarter of a century of intensive clinical practice devoted primarily to the treatment of the suicidal. In this work I will present the procedures and training required of the therapist, describe the rewards in the treatment of the suicidal elderly, and encourage you, the clinical therapist, to do the same.

Suicide in the elderly is both a widespread problem and the subject of widespread misapprehensions. In this introduction I present seven of the most prominent misunderstandings, and my response to these distortions. They represent the lack of knowledge and the presence of un-examined attitudes that form one of the major reasons for writing this book. These misunderstandings will be further clarified in the chapters on theory, recognition, assessment, and treatment.

The first misunderstanding is the belief that elderly suicide is a minor problem compared to other populations. For example, surveys of atti-tudes and information regularly reflect the belief that the suicide rate is higher in the young (e.g., Domino, 1991). The fact is that the elderly com-prise the highest risk group for suicide.

The elderly suffer more losses, illnesses, blows to self-esteem, and al-together more of the experiences that have been statistically associated with suicide than any other group. The fact that there are not more sui-cides among the elderly is a tribute to their resources, the strengths of their social and emotional support systems, and the affirmation of life-oriented attitudes. It is because of these resources and strengths that eld-erly suicide is treatable. The elderly deserve credit for surviving, not criticism and rejection for being alive.

A second belief is that being ill when one is old is a good enough rea-son for suicide. This belief has been frequently espoused by the news media and by the publications of euthanasia organizations, joined by the exhortations of such public figures as former Governor Richard Lamm of Colorado and such books as *Common Sense Suicide* (Portwood, 1978).

However, the idea that illness is a sufficient reason for suicide goes counter to all my experience in treating depression and suicide. The rea-sons for suicide in the elderly always involve conditions other than ill-ness itself; illness alone is never a sufficient reason.

The third belief is that biomedical advances are a curse with no re-deeming features. They keep people artificially alive and miserable. In fact, the advances in the biological sciences have the potential to en-hance the quality of life. It is unfortunate that it is often presented as an obstacle to be overcome.

The movement to hasten dying finds many more adherents in the me-dia than the approval of survival in the face of adversity. For example, a page one article in the July 19, 1989, *New York Times* discussed the rise in the elderly suicide rate and attributed some of the increase to medical progress, leading to elderly people living—or rather, dying—longer. What might be considered a follow-up article six days later discussed the legal and medical ramifications of turning off life supports for the comatose. An opposing view has never reached page one of the *Times*.

Another example is the book, *This Far and No Farther*, by Andrew Mal-com, and the movie made from it called "The Right to Die," about Emily

Bauer. Mrs. Bauer had amyotrophic lateral sclerosis (ALS), otherwise known as Lou Gehrig's Disease. She chose to die and made this choice after being rejected by her family. Meanwhile, her husband turned away from her and found someone else. However, the reason for her decision was presented as based solely upon her illness. The fact that her husband, children, and other family members had to adjust and find new ways of keeping the family intact, and that they did not do so, was ignored. Blind spots are particularly prevalent in those who will not see, because to see means the acceptance of unaccustomed changes in their roles and behavior.

There are many cases that are very different from that of Emily Bauer. For example, one woman wrote to the newsletter of "The Society for the Right To Die," about her mother who had come down with the same illness. The family expected her to choose death and were willing to accommodate her. However, the lady continued to enjoy being with her family and seeing her grandchildren grow. She coped effectively with her growing neurological and muscular impairments, which were as severe as Emily Bauer's. The relatives must also have accepted their ill mother as she was and adjusted their behavior accordingly.

Other examples include Stephen Hawking, progressively impaired physically after 16 years of ALS. That did not keep him from becoming one the the world's leading physicists and the author of the best-seller, *A Brief History of Time*. Richard Ellmann, the late author of the definitive biographies of Oscar Wilde and James Joyce, continued working on his monumental studies until the very end, despite the ravages of his disease. The documentary film, "One More Season," was about a football coach who continued to work and be respected and affirmed despite his being ill with ALS. Senator Jacob Javits is another member of this distinguished company. When he was treated for ALS at Mt. Sinai Hospital in New York City, he was an inspiration to the other patients and the entire staff, being cheerful and responsive to the end.

Once I was talking with a proponent of euthanasia, who gave the case of Emily Bauer as an example of suicide as a rational response to ALS. I mentioned Javits and his courage and good cheer as a role model for all ages. She shrugged away his example with, "Well, he was an exceptional person," as though that kept him from being an acceptable role model for us unexceptional, ordinary beings.

She may not have known of the work of Bernie Siegel (1986) and others, who celebrated those "exceptions" among cancer patients, who fought and overcame their illness. It is the exceptions who are to be admired, not those who celebrate death, and like Derek Humphry hand out lethal pills to their friends (Gabriel, 1991).

There are many more such "exceptional" persons in the world, unsung and quietly courageous. In conferences and forums where I have presented examples, members of the audience have invariably approached me to describe similar experiences in their own families. Nevertheless, for many in the euthanasia movement, it is as though only negative and death-oriented solutions are acceptable in the face of aging or disability, while courage and the affirmation of life are deviations to be explained away.

How one lives and dies is the true Living Will that is handed down to future generations. Life can be affirmed, even in those situations where suicide is most frequently applauded by the advocates of euthanasia. Medical advances have not only saved lives but helped enrich the lives of those who survive, including the elderly who had attempted suicide, and permitted many of them to return to a condition of well-being and satisfaction in life. Medical progress is also a blessing.

Those who see medical advances as an unmitigated disaster overlook the fact that old age is a time of high morale and high satisfaction in living for most older people. This feeling of well-being is based upon psychological factors, positive relationships with others, the presence of Social Security and other provisions to help the elderly be more independent, and those very medical advances under attack, which have helped them continue to function and be active.

Fourth is the belief that the elderly drain the social resources that are needed for infants and children. By surviving, they harm the rest of society. The elderly do so, according to these critics, because ours is a deficit economy with scarce material and personal resources. The belief that what is good for the old is bad for the young places the generations in an unnecessary and invalid conflict.

Fifth is the attitude that suicide in an older person is for the best. Literature and the media present the elderly as miserable, ill, alone, alienated, and rejected by society, as well as a burden to their families, to themselves, and to others, with suicide as the most desirable solution. These sources see the elderly as unproductive, of no value to themselves or anyone, useless, unloved, unwanted, and a drain on the economy.

The belief that suicide is for the best disregards at least four facts: (a) When people are suicidal they are expressing a problem in living. The solution is not to put an end to life. That would be like blowing up the school house because of a difficult problem in arithmetic. It is more sensible to find and solve the problem. (b) Most suicidal elderly persons are very ambivalent about suicide. (c) Elderly suicide may be destructive to the survivors. Suicide is a death that can rarely be mourned appropriately and often results in long-standing emotional and behavioral disturbances. It is a legacy handed down from one generation to the next. (d) Regarding the consistent evidence that the elderly *are* loved.

Nevertheless, many professionals continue to believe in the suicide solution for the elderly, often on the incongruous grounds of compassion, combined with the desire to save money. Examples include a prominent rabbi who hailed the suicide of Sigmund Freud as "The rational and moral action to take" (Reines, 1991). (For more information on Freud's suicide see Max Schur, *Freud: Living and Dying* and Vol. II of Jones' biography.) One psychoanalyst wrote approvingly of the suicide of Bruno Bettelheim, one of the foremost analysts of our times, quoting the poem, "Death be not proud/But proud be those/Who met their death/At the time they chose" (Caruth, 1991). Such approval may be related to the finding that a high suicide rate is present in mental health professionals in general, and psychoanalysts in particular. Bettelheim was only the most recent example, joining Freud, William Stekel, Victor Tausk, Paul Federn, and many others.

If you should happen to be old, ill, and depressed, watch out, even if you are as prominent as Bruno Bettelheim. An editorial in a nursing journal reports that he was at a party, looking very unhappy, shortly before his suicide. A man who did not know him struck up a conversation, and Dr. Bettelheim told him that he was depressed. The man's response was, "Have you heard of the Hemlock Society?" That was certainly a pro-suicide, anti-age response that would not have been given to a younger person. If Dr. Bettelheim had told the man he had financial problems, would his response have been, "Have you heard of the poorhouse"? Perhaps suicide is the poorhouse of the despairing elderly.

The sixth belief, also prevalent in the professional community, is that the suicidal elderly do not respond to psychotherapy. The alleged "findings" in the literature on the assessment and treatment of the suicidal lead to the recommendation of psychotherapy for younger suicidal persons but not for the older. For them, the recommendation is for medication, shock treatment, and institutionalization. These recommendations against psychotherapy for the elderly preceded the recent movement by Callahan (1987) and others to limit their physical medical care.

The bias against psychotherapy for the suicidal elderly in the professional community is related, in part, to a misunderstanding of the aging process, including Sigmund Freud's belief that older persons were not amenable to his form of treatment. I will have much more to say about this professional misunderstanding.

A second source of professional resistance is what may be called premature euthanasia, a too hasty conclusion that an elderly person is ready for his or her conclusion. That, in turn, is based in equal parts upon the inadequate training of health professionals in the treatment of the elderly and their failure to come to terms with ageism and their own fears of illness and death.

Misunderstandings have also been perpetuated by eminent leaders in the field. Often, those who write our professional books are academics or researchers who do not treat the ones they write about. The conclusions they draw from their studies are based upon inference and sometimes false logic, rather than actual studies of psychotherapy. A major component is an underestimation by professionals of the assets of the elderly. However, it is fortunate that there are others who have devoted themselves to studying and treating the suicidal elderly in a more understanding manner.

The seventh belief is the emphasis upon death as a right which must be upheld for the elderly. Publications on the right to die for the elderly far outweigh the right to live, with *Final Exit* (Humphry, 1991) but one of many. My disagreement is with the emphasis, not the right.

Those laboring for the right to die forget that the living also have rights, and these people rarely labor to improve the conditions of the elderly that lead to suicide. There are some distinguished exceptions, such as Ann Wickett, the estranged wife of Derek Humphry, the founder of the Hemlock Society. He left her when she developed breast cancer, after which she committed suicide. She was one of the rare writers for euthanasia who displayed empathy and compassion for the anguish that leads elderly persons to commit suicide. In her last book, she emphasized that "Above all, the old and sick should be regarded as valuable and worthwhile people, not discards" (Wickett, 1989, p. 9).

The so-called free choice of death is rarely free because of the complex of forces impinging upon the suicidal person. If the right to live is disregarded, then the right to die may become a compulsion to die. The choice of not committing suicide is an affirmation of life, but we hear too little of that for the elderly.

These seven beliefs form the foundations of despair and death in the vulnerable elderly. What is less known is the influence of their suicides upon other age groups. There is a "trickle down" effect, bringing death to the young as well as the old.

The best response to myths and false beliefs is found in experiences in the actual treatment of the suicidal elderly. I have worked intensively and intimately with patients in individual, group, and especially family therapy, and can testify that suicidal elderly men and women can be treated successfully. The task for the therapist is a uniquely rewarding one. But I would never say it was easy.

This volume describes an approach to the treatment of the suicidal elderly that is based upon the affirmation of life. It is a practical work that presents the psychotherapeutic procedures I have found most effective. The major modalities—of crisis intervention, family, group, and individual therapy—are examined in the context of a comprehensive and interdisciplinary approach.

With the proper treatment we can reduce the suffering of the depressed, despairing, and suicidal elderly and help provide them with a life of renewed generativity and integrity. Such results can be achieved even at the end of life, even in those whose life-long experiences have apparently been of failure and rejection. The process is illustrated with many examples, from the initial recognition to assessment and therapy.

The treatment is based upon a solid bedrock of research and studies in the literature as well as over a quarter-century of specialization in working directly with the suicidal. I also include research, experiences, and insights derived from different or younger populations when they were relevant to the elderly suicide. Conversely, the principles of treatment of the suicidal elderly often apply to suicidal persons of all ages. Elderly suicide cannot be understood outside the context of the overall problem of suicide. Consequently, the cases and applications in this book range from children to the very old, and from those with mild suicidal ideation to people who are intent upon ending their lives.

I am concerned with *all* forms of suicide in the elderly, including indirect self-destructive behavior. My primary focus, however, is upon the treatment and prevention of direct suicidal reactions. This book explores some of the major social, biological, situational, and psychological conditions associated with elderly suicide, how to recognize the strengths and assets of the elderly, as well as the foundations of theory, assessment, and practice for the therapist.

Preventing Elderly Suicide

Overcoming Personal Despair,
Professional Neglect,
and Social Bias

1

Demography and the Theoretical Foundations of Elderly Suicide

As yet a child, nor yet a fool to fame;
I lisped in numbers, for the numbers came.

—Alexander Pope

Professional assessment requires a thorough and comprehensive evaluation, and some knowledge of its theoretical rationale. The areas covered in the following chapters on assessment and treatment are derived from different disciplines, from biology to the humanities. For the purpose of understanding and treating the suicidal, the findings associated with an affirmation of life are emphasized and then contrasted with those characteristics that encourage a disconfirmation of life and a suicidal state.

An evaluation of assets and resources is included as well as risk factors, for a valid diagnosis is a basis for treatment, and must therefore be thorough. As we shall see in Chapter 2, diagnosis is not therapy, but it is nevertheless therapeutic. For the suicidal, assessment and treatment merge and are intertwined.

DANGER SIGNS AND RECOVERY FACTORS

The reasons for suicide are not as self-evident as they may seem on the surface, and demographic information provides a valuable background. Within the context of suicidal behavior, demography means the scientific collection and study of the social statistics of populations where suicide occurs. The term refers to groups and societies, not individuals. Nevertheless, we need this information to understand individuals.

Demographic data are often surprisingly relevant to individuals who are at risk. The French sociologist Emile Durkheim concluded, purely on the basis of statistics, that the breakdown of social cohesion was the basic component of the social suicide rate. That conclusion is not only a contribution to social theory, but has also saved lives. Social cohesion is the basis of psychotherapy with the suicidal elderly, as I practice it. (For more on Durkheim see below.)

The elderly constitute the group with the highest suicide rate in the United States and most of the European and Western countries (McIntosh, 1992). This has been true since the beginning of the 20th century, and it remains true today as we approach the 21st century. Such information is familiar to most gerontologists, but not to the general public. Studies have shown a prevailing belief that the suicide rate is highest in young people. The truth concerning that belief is that the suicide *attempt* rate is highest in the young and low in the elderly.

For the practical prediction and potential prevention of suicidal behavior, the major demographic, epidemiological, and recognition signs are placed together in Table 1.1, followed by a discussion of their meaning, theoretical rationale, and clinical implications. (An outline of family danger signs is provided in Table 5.1, below.) These indicators are intimately related to the conditions, both conscious and unconscious, overt and covert, associated with elderly suicide. Very broad factors as age, sex, and ethnic origin are omitted. The indicators refer primarily, although not exclusively, to present rather than past conditions. However, previous suicide attempts, and a history of suicide in the family, are of such import that they were included.

The recognition signs summarized in Table 1.1 combine direct experiential events with demographic indicators. They comprise a body of data that could be of value for everyone, not only professionals. The knowledge of how to respond to these danger signs is as important as the ability to recognize the danger signs themselves.

Table 1.1
Recognition and Recovery Factors: The Most Frequent Signs

I. Ego Weakening Factors

Major mental, physical, or neurological illness.
Depression.
Paranoia or a paranoid attitude.
Alcoholism or heavy drinking.
Intractable, unremitting pain, mental or physical, that is not responding to treatment.

II. Social Isolation

Living alone.
Living in the inner city, or a socially disorganized area.
Few or no friends.
Isolation or social withdrawal of a couple.

III. Psychodynamic Factors

A major loss, such as the death of a spouse.
A history of major losses.
A recent suicide attempt.
A previous history of suicide attempts.
A family history of suicide.
Major crises or transitions, such as retirement or imminent entry into a nursing home.
Major crises or changes in others, especially among family members.
Age-related blows to self esteem, such as loss of income or loss of meaningful activities.
Loss of independence, when dependence is unacceptable.

IV. Attitudinal and Communication Factors

Rejection of help; a suspicious and hostile attitude towards helpers and society.
Expressions of feeling unnecessary, useless, and devalued.
Increased irritability and poor judgment, especially following a loss or some other crisis.
Expression of the belief that one is a burden, in the way, or harmful to others.
Expression of the belief that one is in an insoluble and hopeless situation.
The direct or indirect expression of suicidal ideation or impulses. Included, too, are symptomatic acts, such as giving away valued possessions, storing up medication, and buying a gun.
Feelings of hopelessness and helplessness in the family and social network.
Feelings of hopelessness in the therapist or other helpers, or a desire to be rid of the patient.
Feelings of being trapped with no way out, and finished with life.
Acceptance of suicide as a solution.

Continued

Table 1.1   Continued

V. Recovery Factors: Resources and Abilities

A potential for:
  Understanding,
  Relating,
  Benefitting from experience, and
  Benefitting from knowledge.
  Acceptance of help.
A potential or capacity for:
  Loving,
  Wisdom,
  A sense of humor,
  Social interest,
  A caring and available family,
  A caring and available social network,
  A caring, available, and knowledgeable professional and health network.

FAMILY RISK FACTORS

The family is potentially the most effective resource for recognizing and responding to the danger signs and thus preventing suicide. However, the family may consist of people who are too enmeshed, and unable to see the situation clearly. The following brief list will summarize family characteristics and show their relationship to the general context of demographic and other recognition indicators.

1. At a time of crisis, suicidopathic families have great difficulty dealing with separation and loss, which are perceived as a threat to the survival of the family system and its traditions.
2. The problem involves not only separation but the symbiotic nature of the family relationships. Symbiosis is characterized by the polarized extremes of either merging and the resulting loss of boundaries, or extrusion and isolation of a family member. The elderly suicidal person is often trying to prevent separation, while other family members are striving to move away towards further separation.
3. The family clings to primary attachments, particularly parents, grandparents, and siblings, with later or secondary relationships seen as a threat to primary relationships.

4. A disturbance in the mourning process is endemic in families that are prone to suicidal reactions and other disturbances. The result is an inability to deal constructively with illness in an elderly family member, with a still further exacerbation of anger, rejection, avoidance, or abandonment.

5. In the closed family system the family seals itself off from an outside world, which they consider a threat to survival.

6. Role conflicts leading to strain and failure are part of a family system of role obligations and functions which can become severely strained with the age-related changes of a vulnerable older member.

7. Maladaptive interpersonal relationships are prominent, the major forms including scapegoating, double binding, ambivalence, and sadomasochistic behavior patterns. A major problem consists in the tendency of the vulnerable elderly person to repeat these patterns outside the family.

8. Affective disturbances permeate all the areas covered in Tables 1.1 and 5.1 on individual and family risk factors.

   From a family perspective the expression and discharge of affect in suicidal persons and their families are rules-governed phenomena. One of the major errors of a one-sided emphasis upon biology is to see drives, instincts, and emotions as purely neurophysiological processes. A more holistic view is that the expression and discharge of emotions and drives are a function of family rules, which are part of a system of roles and expectations (Jackson, 1965).

   For example, a father may be domineering, bullying, and violent at home, while the wife and children are weak and submissive. At work, the same father may be passive and unassertive. The well known "pecking order" is another example of the rules governed expression of aggression.

9. Communication disturbances include indirect, devious, selective, and destructive messages, combined with a marked tendency toward secretiveness.

10. Suicidopathic families are prone to frequent and unresolved crises which, because they are unresolved, pile stress upon stress until the tension reaches unbearable levels.

11. The family assessment and treatment process follows the road from separation intolerance to crisis intolerance. Most frequently there is an early dramatic decrease in tension and separation anxiety, followed by a resumption of growth and mature development. This description may be deceptive. The process is a

rocky one, by no means as smooth as suggested here. Nevertheless, its success is based upon understanding and confronting the
family factors summarized in Table 5.1.

Tables of demographic and recognition signs generally include indi-
ces of danger or risk, as is proper. Since an adequate evaluation must
include the resources for overcoming the suicidal state, Table 1.1 also
includes 12 resources and strengths. They are found in those who recover from their suicidal state, and are the same as the principles of all
successful aging.

BIOLOGY AND THE AFFIRMATION OF LIFE

Table 1.1 is organized into five sections. Section I, Ego Weakening Factors, contains a small but powerful list of conditions that are largely, although not exclusively, biological in their origin or effects. What follows
is the theoretical underpinning of these conditions.

As used here, biology refers to the functional and structural components of human physiology and anatomy including neurological, consti-
tutional, and genetic factors. Biological stress often precipitates a
suicidal state. In major depression and other illnesses, for example, the
biological components may be prominent, although rarely exclusive as
the individual, the social, or the family can all be seen as contributory.
Biology does not exist in a social or psychological vacuum.

Beginning with the discovery of thorazine in the early 1950s, and the
resulting dramatic improvement in the condition of many schizophrenics, biomedical therapy has been extended to depression, anxiety, pho-
bias, panic states, and obsessive-compulsive disorders with fruitful
results. Biological advances, also known as "The biomedical revolution"
(Veatch, 1976), have been praised and damned. They have been hailed
as a breakthrough in the treatment and understanding of medical and
psychiatric disturbances, and criticized as presenting a one-sided and
inadequate picture of treatment and the nature of the human organism.

The emphasis upon the biological has been denounced for its exces-
sively narrow focus. As Dumont (1991) said in his critique, biological
psychiatry claims that the mind can be studied independent of a social
context. "It fails to recognize that context is complex and in itself, worthy
of study with at least as much relevance to issues of mental health and
illness as the individual brain" (p. 4).

An overemphasis upon biological treatment can be counterproductive and, paradoxically, based upon nonbiological, social and economic considerations. Breggin (1991), for example, saw many of the problems in psychiatric treatment as exacerbated by a collusion between the pharmaceutical establishment and the psychiatric profession. That criticism is particularly applicable to the treatment of the elderly, where "the biomedicalization of gerontology" (Kane, 1991), has led to a relative disregard of social and psychological factors in the aged.

My own experience indicates that biological therapy is valuable and often necessary, in the context of a thorough and flexible treatment plan. A therapist who ignores what biology has to offer is not a competent therapist. However, to administer medication without regard to the doctor–patient relationship or the social situation of the patient is to practice bad medicine.

The effects of biological or genetic disorders can be modified by life events or psychological treatment. Some people who are mentally retarded, organically disabled, or have other biologically based disorders adjust well, while others do poorly depending upon life experiences and how they are accepted by the family and society. Targum (1988) gives an example of identical twins, both of whom had a bipolar affective disorder. One adapted well and the other did not, the difference being in the nature of their interpersonal experiences and family relationships.

In the families of my suicidal patients, the *fear* of genetic or hereditary disturbances such as insanity or suicide has often been a major source of terror, conflict, and emotional disturbances.

Caroline P., at age 43, was afraid that her son was fated to inherit the condition that led to his paternal grandfather's suicide. She blamed her husband for having such heredity. The grandfather had been singled out as the reason for tensions in the family, but when he put himself out of the way by committing suicide, tensions increased to a dangerous level, with symptoms of depression, suicide, and behavior problems appearing in both the father and the son.

Fears of a biological disorder may precipitate a suicide. Lester (1987) speculated that the worry over an inherited taint may have contributed to the suicide of Marilyn Monroe. She feared she had inherited the defective genes which made her mother and grandmother mentally ill, and that she would also end her days in a mental hospital. Fears of genetic disturbances are not hereditary, but they can be as deadly as the genetic condition itself. Conversely, hope that genetic or other biologically based disturbances can be surmounted or treated can lead to a successful adjustment. The therapist experienced with suicidal persons and their anxieties explores these feelings and attitudes before arbitrarily or automatically prescribing drugs or hospitalization. The most effective therapeutic approach is to recognize the value of the biological as part of the total organism, and to play the role of an educator, explaining the treatment to the patient and the family.

The Unity of the Organism

The psychosomatic point of view posits that all physical reactions have a psychological and social base, and conversely that all psychological and social behaviors contain a biological substratum. For example, recent studies in the emerging field of psychoneuroimmunology (Vollhardt, 1991) have found that positive attitudes improve immune functioning while negative ones inhibit the immune system. In a series of studies, Pennebaker (1990) found that confiding secrets, unburdening oneself to others, or even writing about upsetting experiences was associated with improved immune functioning. These studies of the effect of thoughts and attitudes upon biological conditions expand the implication of the famous statement by Shakespeare's Polonius: "There is nothing either good or bad but thinking makes it so."

Biological Components of the Negation of Life

There has been little written about the ego state of the elderly suicidal person, aside from one-sided descriptions of the declining resources and coping abilities that accompany old age. Gitelson (1975), for example, described the normal aging process as one of regression, increased irritability, and withdrawal.

Freud's description of the ego in melancholia (1957), published over 75 years ago, is still the standard, even though he wrote only peripherally about suicide. He postulated that melancholia, which would now be called a major depression, contains a number of identifiable characteristics. These include a regression from mature object or interpersonal relationships to identification and incorporation, and a turning of energies, especially aggression, against the self. It was perhaps Freud's genius to recognize the degree to which this biological condition was simultaneously psychological and interpersonal.

The symptoms of depression include hypochondriasis, sleep, appetite, and other gastrointestinal disturbances, and fatigue or lassitude.

(The depressive picture is described in more detail in the discussion of the clinical manifestations of suicidal signs, later in this chapter.) In depression there is also a decreased control over drives and when these drives include hostility turned against the self, the accumulated stress and pressures greatly increase the threat of suicide. Finally, when there is no relief from these symptoms, hopelessness and despair take over. These disturbances all lead to a disconfirmation of life. The task of the healer is to replace this disconfirmation with affirmation.

Affirmation and Disconfirmation in Biochemical Advances

The biomedical revolution has prolonged life and permitted a longer period of well-being for millions of elderly men and women. On the other hand, it has kept people artificially alive but in a vegetative state, a result of respirators and other machines that keep them breathing and keep their blood circulating.

As in most biological phenomena, biochemical advances cannot be understood outside of their psychological, family, and social aspects. The medical profession is a particularly vital social, as well as a treatment system. With the decline and virtual demise of the doctor who made house calls and the increasing reliance upon the laboratory as a replacement for the doctor–patient relationship, there has been a progressive dehumanization of medicine.

Many socially-based phenomena are attributed to biochemical advances while neglecting other factors. An example is the reaction to the progressive increase in the elderly suicide rate from 1980 to 1988. This increase occurred after a steady decline from the 1950's through the 1970's. In fact, the literature prior to 1980 usually discussed reasons for the decline in the elderly suicide rate (Resnik & Cantor, 1970; Marshall, 1978).

The news media became interested in elderly suicide in the context of Dr. Jack Kervokian's suicide machine, which he first used to assist Janet Adkins to kill herself and subsequently assisted others. He did this in the name of compassion and mercy, accusing those who opposed him of being "Nazis."

The manner in which the media dealt with the Adkins death is a warning to the public refrain from taking news accounts at face value. *Newsweek*, for example, showed a graph depicting the increase in elderly suicide from 1980 to 1988, the latest year for which such statistics were available. They ignored the decreasing rate during the previous decades, and attributed the increase purely to biochemical advances. Perhaps such news reporting can be attributed to a decrease in editorial responsibility during the last half of the 20th century. (The social context of the increase in the elderly suicide rate is discussed further in the latter part of this chapter.)

What, meanwhile, can be done for the growing numbers of those who are kept artificially alive? There are upwards of 10,000 patients in the United States in a persistent vegetative state. These persons are not only hooked up to machines but are surrounded and cared for by strangers. There is a growing effort in this country to refrain from such artificial biomedical procedures.

The difficulty lies in thinking that doctors can pull the plug or withdraw food and water while the social context remains the same. The problem may lie less in keeping people alive artificially and more in our neglect and abandonment of those in need of care, of which those in a coma or vegetative state are only the most extreme examples. Many such patients could be cared for at home with the help of family and home-care personnel. The cost would be less, and the home is a more natural setting. It is time for the restoration of home and family care as part of medicine.

The chemical aspect of the biochemical equation must also be considered. Chemistry has been a blessing in many ways. The chemical preservation of food, for example, has made possible long-term storage and transportation to great distances and chemistry has thereby prevented illness and death. However, chemistry has also contributed immeasurably to the pollution of our environment and many chemicals are suspected poisonous and carcinogenic agents.

The situation has been humorously depicted by E. B. White (1955) in his science fiction fantasy of a future society where everyone must be injected daily in order to counteract the poisons in food. Today's reality is too close to that situation to be funny any longer. Cattle are injected with hormones to increase their weight. Chickens are similarly treated, their diets filled with chemicals, while lights remain on to keep them laying eggs continuously. E. B. White followed these biochemical measures to their logical conclusion. In his fantasy of the future cows gave milk in a steady stream, day and night, while being propped up and fed intravenously.

In summary, life can be a biological event to be affirmed and celebrated, even while waging a courageous and unceasing battle against the forces of disconfirmation and negation. Problems arise when living becomes laden with anxiety, pain, and other unpleasant feelings precipitated by the events summarized in Table 1.1. Help is available, provided by the much maligned biomedical advances.

No one functions optimally to their fullest extent. However, with the help of others, even those with paralysis can attain what Peck (1975) called "body transcendence." People with amyotrophic lateral sclerosis, or Lou Gehrig's Disease, can enjoy the stimulation of sights, sounds, taste, and other senses, even if only through an affectionate touch and a loving glance. They can be present at family meetings and other events and be greeted with affection and joy. If we can affirm life successfully in the teeth of illness and approaching death, then we can affirm it anywhere. Long may biological progress continue to advance in the fight for the well-being of humanity.

SOCIAL COHESION VERSUS ALIENATION: THE CONTRIBUTIONS OF SOCIOLOGY

Section II of Table 1.1, on Social Isolation, deals with the person's external situation. The most relevant factors include where and with whom the person lives. Sociology has greatly clarified why this area is so significant for understanding and preventing suicide. Many studies have demonstrated that the suicide rate is related to social conditions. For example, both suicide and homicide rates are correlated with the rise and fall in the business cycle (Henry & Short, 1954). Suicide rates are known to decrease during times of war and increase during times of peace.

The elderly suicide rate also varies in response to social events. For example, elderly suicide decreased with the onset of social security during the New Deal era, and decreased still further with Medicare. After 1980 the elderly suicide rate again began to climb. The increase took place while Reagan was president, from 1980 to 1988, and appeared to be correlated with threats to such services as Social Security and Medicare and the gradual, though covert, rationing of health care. Hypothetically, the elderly suicide rate can be seen as one index of the social health of society.

Elderly suicide is also correlated with other social ills. Rossi (1990) found a decrease in the rate of homelessness before 1980, followed by an increase in homelessness during the Reagan years. The sequence paralleled the fall and then the rise of suicide rates in the elderly. As Senator Gore (1990, p. 962) noted, "Unfortunately, in the 1980's, there was a retreat from the long-standing commitment to public housing, and the results have been grim."

Such social effects seem associated with both social changes and with the more stable characteristics of a society. Osgood and McIntosh (1986) report that the aged are devalued and their status is lower in technologically advanced cultures. The broader social structure and mores help explain why the suicide rates of the elderly are highest in industrialized countries, such as the United States, Canada, and Europe.

The status of the elderly is higher in some "primitive" societies. But the price they used to pay in other societies was more drastic. For example, it is commonly believed that the Eskimo culture, in order to ensure sufficient food for everyone, would have their elderly commit suicide. Not only the social structure, but simple economics are not always kind to the old. A similar social problem involving an elderly grandmother was presented in Satjat Ray's movie, "Pather Panchali," where she was driven from the house to die.

The Eskimo experience suggests that the elderly are more at risk in deficit societies where there is not enough to go around, *or it is perceived that way.* For example, Medicare, Social Security, and other services for the elderly have been presented in the media recently as depriving the needy young. Portwood (1978) gave a similar argument in her suggestion that the suicide rate among the elderly is too *low.* The attitude, not necessarily the reality, is similar to the reported attitude of the Eskimos.

Where resources are perceived as scarce, the elderly are seen as depriving others; they are encouraged to die and to commit suicide. Where resources such as food, medical care, and housing are perceived as plentiful, the elderly are accepted more and encouraged to live.

Can social variables help explain individual behavior such as suicide? I believe that they contribute significantly to psychological variables such as self-hate among the elderly, elderly-hate among the young, and a disbelief in the worth of human life in the elderly. Four such variables include first, the perception that social measures benefitting the elderly do so at the expense of the young; second, human relationships are depersonalized in large industrial societies; third, there is a lack of appreciation and recognition of the wisdom, experience, and other assets of the elderly; and fourth, there is an excessive emphasis upon materialistic values.

The devaluation of the aged seems greater in societies where people are valued for their material usefulness, and not simply for themselves. Portwood (1978), for example, argued in favor of suicide for the elderly because they do not produce, and are of little or no worth materially. If Jesus of Nazareth had followed such reasoning, he would have banned the lilies of the field because "They toil not, neither do they spin."

In less industrialized countries older people may be valued more for what they are or what they symbolize to the culture and its traditions. It follows that the elderly are valued more in societies where material resources are perceived as sufficient for everyone, and where relations are more direct, with people more in contact with each other. Lack of contact is characteristic of larger units, in the big cities, for example. Those living alone and socially isolated are the least valued, and the most at risk for suicide.

These findings call for a change in social attitudes. Osgood and McIntosh also note that "The elderly in this society are often viewed as useless, dependent, nonproductive, and a burden to be borne by young members. . . . Their wisdom and experience . . . are not valued. The implication for the restoration of hope for the despairing elderly at risk for suicide is to recognize and value their wisdom and experience" (1986, p. 7). The treatment of the suicidal elderly begins with the healing attitude and acceptance of the therapist, but also of society.

The high suicide rate in elderly white males has been consistently related to their loss of status, role, power, and money. Many suicides are committed by people who valued themselves and were valued by others on the basis of their wealth, status, power, and control. The further implication is that suicide prevention calls for a change in values, from an emphasis upon success and material accumulations to a more altruistic and spiritual emphasis.

DURKHEIM AND HIS CONTRIBUTION

Durkheim has been the major sociological contributor to the understanding of suicide, comparable to Freud in the psychological realm. His book on suicide was published at approximately the same time as Freud's *Interpretation of Dreams*, at the beginning of the 20th century. Let us hope that the inauguration of the 21st will be as great a period of creative stimulation and ferment.

Using extensive demographic data from various countries and societies, Durkheim concluded that the suicide rate varies inversely with the degree of integration of the person. That is, those most at risk are those least integrated, most alienated, with a feeling of not belonging. (And I add, those at risk are the ones with the greatest need for acceptance and belonging, especially within the family.)

Durkheim dealt with institutions and society, especially the role of social integration and cohesion. However, just as Freud's analytic theories contain challenging social implications, Durkheim's sociological theories contain intriguing implications for individual suicides. By combining the theories of Freud, Bowlby, Erikson, and Durkheim, the implications for an effective integrative therapy of suicide are enormous. Durkheim helps explain how social cohesion contributes to the power of the treatment modalities. To quote Osgood and McIntosh (1986), "persons who are deeply and intimately involved with others in various social groups should be low suicide risks."

In the suicidal elderly the decrease in integration seems related to the weakening and loss of various social roles, the loss or unavailability of significant relationships through death or moving, and dynamic reasons such as conflicts. A decrease in family integration combined with an increase in family conflict is a major pattern associated with both suicide and role loss. And our society is structured so as to deprive the elderly of significant life roles while not providing replacements.

The loss of status by the elderly who are vulnerable to suicide can result in disgust and despair rather then ego integrity. As Beck and his colleagues (1979) noted in their work on the cognitive theory of depression, an older person in a state of severe depression and grief may find the entire past and future colored by these current feelings. In other words, disgust and despair in the suicidal elderly is a basis for treatment, not for giving up. The goal of treatment would be the replacement of these negative feelings with social cohesion and a feeling of belonging, as well as an increase in self-esteem and social engagement.

Integration, or ties with other people, is more than a social phenomenon; it is part of a dynamic situation, based upon the transactional interplay of individuals and groups. Cohesion is related to unity, harmony between peoples, and ultimately, the brotherhood of man, which is the basis of true community.

An example of striving for such community was provided by Louis Adamic, an immigrant to the United States who, in the 1930's, helped organize "The Common Council for American Unity." Part of their program was "to help create among the American people the unity and mutual understanding resulting from a common citizenship . . . to further an appreciation of what each group has contributed to America . . . to overcome intolerance and discrimination because of foreign birth, descent, race, or nationality . . . to help the foreign-born and their children solve their special problems of adjustment" (Adamic, 1942). Essentially, those are the goals that need to be revived today, emphasizing mutual respect and appreciation of other peoples and cultures. That is the greatest application of Durkheim to society. Multiculturalism starts with the integration of a once alienated people within the larger society, and that begins with the individual and the intimate social network or group.

Finally, there is the affirmation of the family and, as in all the other areas, the affirmation is reciprocal. Self-affirmation is associated with positive affect and experiences in the family, while disconfirmation is associated with negative experiences.

The early writings and experiments of the gestalt psychologists (Ellis, 1938) and their reflections in neurology and psychiatry (Goldstein, 1939), may contribute further to the greater understanding of cohesion. Just as the organism is one, the family, society, the world, and the universe form one grand unified gestalt.

Addressing the combination of the biological, psychological, and social forms the basis for the fundamental goals of treatment of the suicidal. Treatment is directed towards all these areas, with the belief that an individual is part of an indivisible organic unit.

PSYCHOLOGY AS AN AFFIRMATION OF THE SELF

Section III of Table 1.1, The Psychodynamic Factors, includes feelings, relationships, and the concrete experiences of the person at risk as well as those who are important in that person's life or death. The psychological contributions range from introspective studies to objective observation, from psychoanalysis to behavior therapy.

The major contributor to the psychological understanding of suicide is Sigmund Freud, who emphasized the intrapsychic, to some extent the interpersonal, and (in his concept of the Oedipus complex) the family. It was left to later investigators to build upon his ideas, even while some rejected them. In his later theorizing the instinctual component became uppermost in the form of the life instinct or eros, which is opposed by the death instinct or thanatos. The death instinct, hypothesized as a striving of all organic matter to become inanimate, was also hypothesized as a fundamental component of suicide.

His psychoanalytic theories included the biologically oriented ego and drive components, which have already been discussed. In this section, his contributions to an understanding of suicide as a problem of the self is combined with other seminal thinkers, notably Erikson, who presented the dialectic interplay between the self and social forces throughout the life span.

In *Mourning and Melancholia* (1957), originally published in 1917, Freud described a regression from object relationships to identification and introjection. The loved one is incorporated, swallowed as it were.

> Mrs. M., was a 62-year-old woman who came to the clinic with the complaint of a compulsive craving for sweets. Her weight had always been within normal limits, but she had gained 42 pounds in the past 6 months. In therapy she soon realized that she was approaching the age at which her mother died from the complications of severe diabetes. Her symptoms of craving sweets and gaining weight were understood as a dynamically motivated regression to incorporation. The identification with her mother was combined with guilt at being well and outliving this beloved figure, precipitating her current depressive episode, and the unconscious effort to become ill in the same way as did her mother.

The establishment of mature relationships is part of a confirmation of the self. In the case of Mrs. M., incorporation represented its disconfirmation. Sometimes, however, incorporation is not a disconfirmation but the only means available for maintaining contact, and can even be a indication of caring.

> Ruth N., a 19-year-old suicidal woman, recalled a dream she had when she was 5. Her mother was a psychotic woman who abused her severely to the point that her life was endangered. Ruth was very empathic and understanding, as little children often are, and very protective of her mother. In her dream at age 5 her mother had become very small, the size of a tiny doll. Her daughter swallowed her and said, "Now I'll have you with me always." (Described in Richman, 1986.)

In this case, incorporation was the only means the daughter had of maintaining the relationship. Her mother had not achieved the level of permitting mature, growth-encouraging relationships with her daughter. Through incorporation the daughter maintained the relationship. She was also protecting her mother, a role which was still her primary one when she entered therapy.

The importance of separation and the resulting anxiety was presented by Freud and Rank, and convincingly affirmed by Bowlby. All these investigators recognized the profoundly disruptive effects of early separation, resulting in insecurity and threats to the mother–infant attachment. Experience with depressed and suicidal people reveals that it is not the separation but the separation anxiety and its association with death that is the problem. There are also examples in the literature from literary figures who are especially gifted with insight and eloquence. Elizabeth Swados (1991) recalled her distress when her mother became severely depressed and suicidal. She tried to remove herself from the family, especially her mother, but her efforts did not work. "I struggled along with my mother inside my self, and as she became more distant and introverted, I began to think hungrily about dying" (p. 109). She turned to her writing, and made a song cycle of Sylvia Plath's Ariel. "I didn't consciously realize that my cycle fitted in perfectly with my mother's suicidal mood. I didn't even put together that Sylvia Plath and my mother had the same first name."

In all these examples of incorporation of an ill or suicidal mother, three features stand out. The first is that the processes of identification and incorporation occur outside of the person's conscious awareness and control. The second is that the incorporation is fundamentally an act of love combined with a deep desire to be with the mother who is in trouble. The third is that the function of incorporation is to prevent separation.

Bowlby (1969, 1973), in particular, demonstrated the affirmative nature of attachment and the disconfirmation resulting from disruptive separations and losses. He presented convincing evidence that separation and attachment are central tasks in the development of life, not only in humans but throughout the animal kingdom. Separation and attachment are biological and social as well as psychological phenomena.

Margaret Mahler and her colleagues (1975) deepened our understanding of separation in human development. She traced the development of the human infant from autism to symbiosis to separation-individuation, and finally to individuation. Her formulations suggest that the seeds of the adolescent's striving for a self are present at a very early age, becoming most evident during the separation-individuation phase. When the transition is not successful, the individual is disconfirmed, autonomy is surrendered, and a regression to earlier stages occurs. Following Mahler's theories, Litman and Tabachnick (1968), hypothesized that suicide was based upon a regression to the separation-individuation phase of development.

Suicidology as a Developmental Science

Erikson's importance for the understanding of elderly suicide is based upon his extension of the psychoanalytic theory of development to the entire life span. Erikson recognizes the importance of the earliest years without underestimating or ignoring the later developmental crises and tasks. Life is a process with a beginning and an end, with a gestalt and unique rhythm of its own. Each life, therefore, is like a great painting or a musical composition. As in any work of art, to end it prematurely leaves the work eternally incomplete.

There is a time to let go of life; but any artificial, "assisted" means is suspect. Freud's "death instinct," to the extent that it is valid, needs no artificial means. When it is time, the wisdom of the organism will let go.

Most developmental psychologists have recognized the importance of Erikson's contributions. The successful resolution of the developmental crises of life culminate in trust, initiative, competence, industry, mastery, autonomy, individuation, an authentic sense of self, ego identity, affiliation, intimacy, mature interpersonal relationships, a realistically positive attitude, generativity, and ego integrity. All represent a confirmation of the self.

Failure in these life tasks lead to basic distrust, shame, doubt, identity diffusion, isolation, stagnation, disgust, and despair. These all represent a disconfirmation of the self. With success the self is confirmed from birth to death while with failure the self is disconfirmed.

Erikson was sensitive to the social and interpersonal components of development, beginning with the first task of development—trust versus basic distrust. Trust is based upon the availability of the mother, and the awareness by the infant that the mother will appear even when temporarily absent. "Smiling crowns this process" (Erikson, 1950, pp. 14–15). It is significant, too, that the origin of trust in smiling is also the origin of humor and good humor, and with that, a positive attitude towards the world. Basic trust is accompanied by basic optimism. The affirmation of life originates in sharing good feelings together.

Basic mistrust arises in the context of insecurity and uncertainty over the parents' presence, both the mother and the father. If they are physically or emotionally unavailable, the seeds of basic mistrust are planted. Basic mistrust, in turn, is intertwined with separation anxiety.

Trust changes with age. The younger generation turns trustingly to the older generation. One task associated with generativity is to live up to that trust. That may require a total commitment, even unto death. When an old person gives up on life and commits suicide, there may be a ripple effect in succeeding generations. Trust may be replaced by disillusionment and distrust, and a resort to suicide in the young.

Investigators have paid relatively scant attention to the later stages. The last two stages of life, when successfully traversed, lead to generativity and ego integrity. Generativity includes being the teachers and models for the younger generation. Ego integrity involves looking at one's life and tying it all together into a meaningful gestalt.

There is another facet of Erikson's theory that deserves special mention. The eight stages do not arise consecutively to subside and to be replaced by the stages that follow. Instead, they continue throughout the life span and continue to develop. At each developmental crisis, of youth, of middle age, old age, and the final or terminal stage, there is a resurgence of the adolescent identity crisis. However, these developmental crises are not the same at different ages.

One further implication of successful development, as presented by Erikson, is the growth of social interest, as described by Alfred Adler. Adler suggested that altruism belongs with work and love as the full measure of maturity and successful adjustment. The concept of social interest can be considered another, and very welcome, bridge between the individual and the social, to replace the "me generation" and the emphasis upon self-interest. With successful therapy, the once suicidal elderly engage more in volunteer work and related activities.

There is a question, however, concerning the value of studying development throughout life for those who are going to specialize in work with children, say, or the elderly. Whatever contributes to suicide at one age may do so for another; whatever prevents suicide at one age may do so for another. That becomes clearly evident in both family and group therapy.

There is an ironic twist to the recent upsurge of interest in euthanasia for the ill elderly: Those who most approve of suicide as a result are the young (Boldt, 1987). Others see such findings as a message for collaborative research and treatment. A recent symposium compared group approaches to the treatment of children at risk for suicide with the treatment of the suicidal elderly (Richman, Brooks, Carter, & Ross, 1991). There were dramatic similarities in treatment approaches and the themes and conflict areas that arose. Age-related differences were also present. Our experience suggested that more such collaborative work, comparing different generations of suicidal persons, can contribute significantly to both theory and practice.

What happens to one generation influences other generations. A dramatic example of the interrelatedness of suicide between generations was reported briefly in the news media but given little attention, just before the great publicity given to Dr. Jack Kervokian. There was an epidemic of four suicides in the high school of a small town in Alabama. One of the dead was a teenage boy whose grandfather had shot himself in the temple, 2 months earlier. The grandson killed himself in the identical manner, with a gun, shooting himself in through the temple.

Such events so convincingly illuminate the ties between generations that they deserve much wider publicity. They contain implications for prevention, vastly more valuable than Kervokian death machines and how-to, final exit books for those contemplating suicide.

All who work with the families of suicidal people know that the suicide of a significant figure can have profound and destructive effects upon different generations. A major loss, crisis, or some other catastrophe, for example, has a far-reaching and reciprocal effect. That is why the therapist for the suicidal must be a life span developmental psychologist, familiar with the tasks, crises, roles, and relationships required from birth to death.

In summary, the treatment of the suicidal elderly is based upon the need for the affirmation of life, for the breakdown of affirmation is a source of stress and despair. The treatment approach described in this book proposes to replace negative attitudes or disconfirmation, with positive attitudes or affirmation. The danger signs of suicidal potential consist of whatever inhibits or limits affirmation, while the recovery signs include everything that increases affirmation. The next section is an introduction to the clinical implications of this comprehensive and life-affirming view.

A CLINICAL OVERVIEW

Section IV of Table 1.1 is on Attitudes and Communication. In the literature these are most often described as clinical recognition and danger signs. Many volumes have been written about the most important of the risk factors for suicide, such as mental and physical illness. This section discusses some of the most prominent indicators with their behavioral, symptomatic, and dynamic features. Their theoretical base has been discussed earlier in this chapter.

Depression

Depression is one of the most frequent conditions associated with suicide and, as is true of most of the significant variables, it is a biopsychosocial condition. It is characterized as an unhappy state, with a low mood, hypochondriasis, vegetative signs such as insomnia, early morning awakening, and gastrointestinal upsets, fatigue, withdrawal, and an inability to perform one's usual activities or meet one's ordinary social role demands.

In the elderly the signs of depression are often disregarded or seen as the manifestations of old age and dementia. They may even be ridiculed and the symptoms "explained" as the natural concomitant of old age. Such an unhappy old person is perceived as a "crock" or a "crank," who is best left alone. As a consequence, the depressive state escalates rather than being treated, and the family and others turn away just when increased emotional and social supports are needed the most.

Fortunately, there are other reactions to a suicidal despair that are more realistic and appropriate, and these have saved many lives. Depression and its accompanying symptoms are communications, just as all other recognition signs are communications, which require a perceptive and sensitive receiver of the communication. When understood and responded to these communications may be life-saving.

Paranoia

There is an interesting reciprocal relationship between depression and paranoia. According to psychoanalytic theory (Freud, 1957), depression is based upon introjection, the process of identification with someone at a very elemental level. The other is swallowed, as it were, and reproaches regarding that person and the love/hate relationship continue, but are turned against the self. Something similar happens in paranoia, through a process of projective identification. A part of one's self, one's own thoughts, feelings, and values, are attributed to or projected onto others.

With severely suicidal persons, depression and paranoia, the processes of both introjection and projection, occur alternately or together. In psychotic persons, where the potential for suicide may be very high, reproaches and complaints are both internalized against the self and projected onto enemies or others, such as an ill-defined "they."

> Anna B., was depressed, withdrawn, and suicidal. She regularly heard voices telling her she was no good and deserved to die; and she alternated between denying the charges and agreeing with them.

These dramatic interplays can best be understood as a dialogue between a projective defense and an introjective surrender.

Projection is an essential component of blaming, which is a universal reaction to adversity that has been called "normal paranoia" by Meissner. It is particularly frequent in families that cannot deal with crises. Sometimes an entire family attributed all its ills to one person within the family. Such scapegoating is frequent after any death, where there is a search to find someone to blame. That occurs with even greater frequency when the death is due to suicide.

> Vilma C.'s brother committed suicide, leaving a wife and five children. The entire family, including Vilma's remaining brother and sisters, their children, wives and husbands, as well as more remote cousins, uncles and aunts, all declared it was Vilma's fault, because she had publicly betrayed a secret involving illicit sexual behavior in the past of the family.

The blaming was a projection, to absolve everyone else in the family from guilt or shame. Unfortunately, the family denied itself the painful but necessary process of self examination and cathartic, healing grieving.

The relationship between paranoia and suicide, as well as other emotional disturbances, is beginning to receive increasing recognition and attention. Allen (1967) saw paranoia as a last ditch defense against suicide. Zigler and Glick (1988) recognized the affective and dynamic roots of projection and other paranoid mechanisms. They postulated that what is diagnosed as paranoid schizophrenia, "may be camouflaged depression and not a true schizophrenia." My clinical observations correspond with both Allen and Zigler and Glick, in that paranoid reactions and symptoms occur as frequently as depressive ones in the suicidal elderly.

Social Isolation

This phenomenon refers to people who are alone *and* alienated. It does not apply to those people who are isolated or without friends, and comfortable in that situation, but only to those with a need for contact and belonging.

In my experience, social isolation is a family phenomenon. With the suicidal elderly, their isolation is the geriatric analogue of "The expendable child," described by Sabbath (1969). They are estranged from their families, who seem to play no discernible role in their lives, or their role in the family is primarily negative, yet they are an intrinsic part of the family system. They usually live apart and alone, but may live with a relative, usually a son or daughter, where they are emotionally and in some cases even physically isolated, remaining in their rooms.

Help Rejection

At the time when a person is in a highly vulnerable state and suicidal, he or she refuses to obtain professional treatment or to accept such help when it is offered. This condition is particularly prevalent among those elderly who are at a very high risk for suicide. Clinical observations suggest three major factors behind such rejection.

First is the sense of stigma attached to being suicidal, and equally or more so to seeing a psychiatrist or other mental health professional, or even to taking anti-depressant or psychotropic medication.

Help-rejecting attitudes are present in other irrationally stigmatized conditions, such as schizophrenia. In a study of suicides among hospitalized schizophrenics (Farberow, Shneidman, & Leonard, 1965) the investigators found that a major group of such suicides were what they called "the unaccepting." Despite their severe and manifest symptoms they insisted they were not ill or suicidal, and refused to enter or cooperate with the treatment program. Their pattern was very similar to that of help-rejecting suicidal persons who are not psychotic or delusional.

A second factor is the presence of parallel attitudes in the family and social network. The relatives are often resistant or opposed to treatment, and at best ambivalent and *double binding*. Double bind communications were first described by Bateson, Jackson, Haley, and Weakland (1956), and observed as frequent in the family interactions at the time of a suicidal state in one of its members. "Characteristic of such interchanges is the presence of one message or directive, together with another message that contradicts the first. Another feature is that the persons involved cannot escape or leave the field. They are therefore trapped . . . Suicide is eventually seen as the only way out" (Richman 1986, p. 162).

In addition to the fear of stigmatization, there is often an identification of the person at risk with a supposedly deranged or suicidal ancestor. Help rejection is often an almost insurmountable obstacle in the treatment of suicidal states. How to deal with suicidal help rejectors is discussed in Chapter 4, "The Healing Relationship."

Similar stigmatizing attitudes are found in some prominent leaders within the organized euthanasia movement. Those who are suicidal and seek help are labeled as "sick." In contrast, to be suicidal and refuse help is presented as a sign of health, and to kill oneself and not obtain help is seen as rational.

A third factor is the inadequate response of the helping professions when elderly people go for help. Haggerty (1973) presented a harrowing account of a 70-year-old man who came to a physician complaining of depression, physical symptoms, sleeplessness, and suicidal feelings. He was given a prescription for sleeping medication, which he promptly used to take an overdose. Thus began a series of meetings with medical and mental health professionals, none of who were sufficiently interested or knowledgeable to provide competent treatment.

This man became depressed and suicidal following the death of his wife. The severity of his reaction and the clear-cut nature of the precipitant cried out for crisis intervention, grief therapy, referral to a widow or widower's group, medication, and perhaps other forms of psychotherapy. At no point, however, were such measures even remotely considered or mentioned, according to Haggerty's report.

It is clear that the rejection of help goes both ways. Help rejection is a social disease as well as an individual problem. It is not only the suicidal elderly who are rejecting help, but society that rejects helping the suicidal elderly.

Alcoholism Or Heavy Drinking

Those who have worked intensively with the suicidal have found that the amount of self-destructive behavior among alcoholics and drug users is pervasive and virtually endemic. As Murphy and Wetzel (1990) among many others have reported, the suicide rate among alcoholics is many times greater than that of the general public. However, the most effective treatment personnel are to be found in the alcoholic community itself.

I spent three years as a consultant on an alcohol ward, one of the very rich teaching and learning experiences of my career. For most of that time I saw patients in multiple group family sessions. I saw that alcoholics and their families who were determined to recover were particularly well suited for helping other alcoholics and families.

I also saw a great affinity between the alcoholic and the suicidal state. One experience that was repeated in a good 40% of the alcoholics was the expression of suicidal threats and attempts while extremely drunk, with a failure to remember these events when they were sober. A suicidal potential was present in these alcoholics, which, at least as a hypothesis, may have predated their alcoholism.

Any change in drinking behavior might be a danger sign. Styron (1990) reported that after drinking steadily for 40 years he developed a sudden intolerance for alcohol and had to stop drinking abruptly. That signaled the onset of a series of events that culminated in an ever increasing major depression and near suicide. No explanation was given for his sudden inability to drink, but whatever the reason, he should have then gone for help. No heavy drinker should stop on his own.

Unremitting Pain

The Los Angeles Suicide Prevention group is to be credited in recognizing that suicide is often preceded by the failure of treatment methods to alleviate both physical pain and psychic pain in the form of depression, grief, remorse, hopelessness, and despair (Shneidman, Farberow, & Leonard, 1970).

The therapist must take care not to enter into that despairing state. It is necessary to realize that unremitting pain is a communication, and the therapist must admit his or her mistakes or errors, while obtaining the consultation and other help that may change the situation and reduce or make the pain bearable.

Loss of Important Others

Separation and loss are implicated in all suicides, at every age. Every suicidal act is, at its core, a reaction to a separation or loss that is believed to be irreparable. A frequent major loss in the elderly is the death of a spouse and/or other emotionally close figure. Losses may begin at a very early age and continue throughout life, with an escalation of such events shortly preceding the suicide.

The problem, however, is not the fact of loss, which is a frequent and universal experience among virtually all the elderly, but how the loss is met. Grief can lead to a rejection of all further strivings or, if the grief process is successfully traversed, to a renewed affirmation of life, the self, and relationships. This matter of loss and separation, and the difficulties with the grief process, are the two most important factors. They are discussed in more detail in the chapter on the family.

Role Change and Loss

This is another area that is discussed in more detail in the family context. Every major developmental and situational change in life requires a re-evaluation of one's status, activities, and obligations in most areas of functioning. In the elderly, these events include widowhood, retirement, loss of job, loss of income, and the effects of mental and physical illness. In many of these cases, roles are lost but not replaced. The results are feelings of being useless, unwanted, and unnecessary. Despair and hopelessness follow almost inevitably. Such role changes occur in the context of the roles of others in the person's family and social network. If the roles of the elderly are not respected or maintained by these, then a suicidal despair may heighten.

Major Illness

Physical, mental, or neurological illness, is a hazardous event which may precipitate a crisis. Early senility, for example, can pose a threat of suicide, especially in someone who had been well-functioning, is still aware of what is happening, and cannot tolerate the implications for future functioning. When an illness is met with panic, hopelessness, helplessness, and despair, it represents a crisis. Crisis intervention is the treatment of choice, the sooner the better, and before assisted suicide is deemed the only intervention.

An illness is not only a biological condition; it is also a communication to the self and others. That applies to hypochondriasis or symptoms without a discernible organic base. After William Styron developed his intolerance for alcohol, he also fell prey to a variety of physical symptoms. He was examined by an internist, who pronounced him physically healthy. It would seem sensible after that to inquire further into the reasons for the symptoms. However, that would have required a broad, comprehensive, multifaceted point of view, which the internist evidently did not possess.

Mr. Styron subsequently developed a severe insomnia. That could be considered another communication of a problem which needed further investigation. Instead, Styron was prescribed Halcion, and advised to take as much as he needed. That was two years before his major depression became overt. It is likely, however, that his intolerance for alcohol and perhaps Halcion, his hypochondriasis, and insomnia, were all prodromal to the depression. The proper attention to these symptoms might have prevented much grief for Mr. Styron and his family.

Other Major Crises in the Self

These crises cannot be separated from the reactions of the family, as well as of the medical professions and other support systems. Many of the elderly patients who eventually committed suicide had exhibited suicidal behavior in the past. For example, Fernando M., described in Chapter 3 on Crisis Intervention, was hospitalized after his suicide attempt at age 70 and discharged after his depression had lifted. However, there was no outpatient follow-up. Had therapy been continued, he might have had help dealing with the loss of his wife. Instead he committed suicide.

Blows to Self-Esteem

These result from a variety of circumstances, some of which have been touched upon as a function of necessary role changes and life changes, such as retirement. An illness can destroy a self, the spiritual even more than the physical. All these cases call for crisis intervention.

Dr. Daniel F. was a noted physician and chairman of a medical department at a highly prestigious medical school. He suffered a debilitating stroke, which forced him to retire and give up his entire career. He committed suicide on the day he was to be replaced as chairman.

Had Dr. F. been honored for his considerable achievements while he was yet alive, perhaps with a Festschrift, a special meeting in his honor, with professional presentations related to his work, and a volume of Proceedings given to him in a public presentation, he might have found it possible to come to terms with his disability. Unfortunately, no one thought of that while he was still alive. On the contrary, he was avoided, because his colleagues found it too painful to see him impaired.

Blows to self-esteem may become unbearable to the person at risk for suicide when family members, friends, or colleagues turn away because they cannot tolerate or accept the disability or illness of a loved one. That is unbearable for the one at risk, even though the turning away may be based upon love. Those who care must not let the former image of the person interfere with their empathy and availability.

Major Crises in Others

More frequently than we realize, an illness, an unresolved problem, the necessity of making an undesired change, or a covert suicidal state in one person can lead to a suicidal, or even homicidal, act in another.

One woman wanted to move closer to her daughter, who had moved to another state and had not invited her parents to come with her. The woman's husband was an alcoholic; she told him she was leaving him because of his drinking, and he attempted suicide.

In a seemingly opposite situation, Mrs. T. had been invited by her daughter to move near her, but she wanted to remain where she was. One night, while brooding about her situation, she suddenly received a revelation that her son, who was a drug addict, had to die. She went to his room and made him swallow an entire bottle of pills. By this focus upon her son, she sought to avoid making a decision regarding her daughter. (From Richman, 1986)

In both cases, the attempts of one person were precipitated by a major crisis in another person. In other cases the results can be more lethal. A major error among some professionals is the failure to appreciate the vast importance of illness and other life changes among family members and the social network.

Edward P., an 80-year-old man, went to see his physician who had prescribed a series of medical tests. "You have cancer and will need an immediate operation," said the doctor. Mr. P. returned home and said to his 60-year-old wife, "The doctor said I have cancer." Mrs. P. said nothing. She went upstairs to the bathroom and there took a fatal overdose of pills.

Sometimes the reverberations of a suicide or some other major crisis are not heard until the next generation.

Frederick T. was successfully treated for cancer but said, nevertheless, that cancer meant death. He committed suicide shortly after. Only then was the secret revealed. When he was a child his mother had committed suicide when told she had cancer. He killed himself using the same method she used.

The family legacy of suicide, which has been hypothesized as a biologically inherited trait, can more fruitfully be seen as a long-term failure to resolve a major crisis, which results in further crises handed down from generation to generation.

Clinical Portents and Communications

These include all the signs and messages that can alert an available and perceptive other to the possibility of a suicidal act. Most relevant are a variety of verbal and nonverbal messages made by the person at risk and sometimes made to the suicidal person by others. Various changes in behavior and personality are included, as are increased drinking, messages that one is a burden, in a hopeless and insoluble situation, that others will soon not have to worry about them, and indicating the presence of a specific plan to commit suicide. Nonverbal messages include giving away valued possessions, hoarding pills, and buying a gun. If these communications occur when the person or couple is socially or psychologically isolated, or when other traumatic events have occurred such as a mugging or series of muggings, then the danger can become extreme.

Section V of Table 1.1, on Recovery Factors, refers to special and inspiring features in the person, the family, and other support networks. They all contribute to recovery from a suicidal state, the increase in life satisfaction and morale, the ability for continued growth, and an affirmation of the self and others.

Chapter 2 places the integration of the demographic and epidemiological data, recognition signs, family characteristics, and recovery factors within a comprehensive and effective assessment process. The chapters that follow describe the treatment procedures in all their rich variety, including how to unlock the constructive forces within elderly suicidal persons and their support systems.

2

Assessment and Early Intervention

A patient was being given the Rorschach. He saw the first card as "A man and a woman having sex," and every other card had the same or similar content. "Why do you have sex on your mind so much?" asked the examiner. "You're the one showing me the dirty pictures," the patient replied.

—*The Folk Wisdom of Jokes*

"Assessment" refers to a clinical evaluation, which includes an accurate awareness by the examiner of the internal conditions, the external situation, and the significant experiences that are relevant to a suicidal state and its recovery. At its best, assessment is systematic, organized, comprehensive, yet flexible. It is not the same as diagnosis, which ordinarily refers to the identification of disease or the classification of people on the basis of their personal or social characteristics (English & English, 1958, p. 150). Diagnosis, however, is part of assessment. As the above joke indicates, assessment is also an interpersonal procedure that includes the relationship with the examiner, and cannot be separated from its context and social implications.

Evaluation is synonymous with assessment, but a more colloquial definition might be "knowing what is going on." That places assessment in league with the other fundamentals of effective therapy. The examiner must possess competent interviewing skills, which include insight and empathy, all of which require sensitive knowledge at both conscious and unconscious levels.

Assessment leads to the formation of a workable treatment plan. The ability to enter into a therapeutic alliance and the formation of an initial and flexible treatment plan are parts of the assessment. A trial period of therapy is one valuable form of assessment.

As the joke illustrates, assessment involves the transference and countertransference reactions that may appear during treatment. The accuracy or failure of assessment may be related to the experience and attitudes of the examiner.

It is evident that assessment is an ongoing process throughout the effective treatment of suicidal people. Theoretically, assessment precedes treatment, but in practice, they work in tandem. Initially, with the suicidal, both assessment and treatment form the basis of crisis intervention.

The interviewing process with the elderly possesses many similarities to the task with younger persons, but there are some special problems that should not be ignored. The examiner has to be familiar with gerontology as well as the principles of interviewing elderly persons. The examiner must be aware of possible sensory deficits in the elderly, such as hearing and vision loss, and how to deal with these during the interview. He or she must adapt to the client's pace and style, not the other way around.

For example, there is the question of interviewing circumstantial or tangential clients. Some elderly people are garrulous and repetitive; they ramble and never get to the point. A premature interruption of the patient by the examiner may be disruptive and inhibit rapport, but a loose, wandering account is equally undesirable. With a combination of proper attention and timing by the therapist, combined with acceptance and accurate empathy, the interview will proceed smoothly and effectively. Some good suggestions for interviewing the ill or impaired elderly are found in Bloom et al. (1971). There is no substitute, however, for direct experience, just as there is no substitute for positive regard.

RECOGNITION OF THE PROBLEM

All assessment starts with the realization that there may be something to assess. As seen in Chapter 1, depression and suicide in the elderly are often overlooked or dismissed as the foibles of old age. An example was Silas P., an 81-year-old hypochondriac in a nursing home who was ridiculed and laughed at for his bowel obsession, until he jumped to his death, and the laughter ceased.

A more positive example was an 86-year-old man in a nursing home, who said his life was over and it was time to die. In this case, however, the depression behind his remarks was recognized, and he was treated successfully.

The death of Silas P. occurred because his caregivers accepted a false stereotype of the elderly person as an acceptable and sufficient explanation of pain or distress. As a result, they saw no need to explore or treat the condition.

The next step, after the awareness that there may be a problem, is determining who does the recognition? The answer is, anyone and everyone who is perceptive enough to see the danger signs, cares enough to want to do something about it, and knowledgeable enough to know how to intervene or where to go for advice or counseling. Knowing what to do or how to respond is as important as recognizing the problem. In the following example, many people saw the danger signs.

> Laura M., a 40-year-old woman, was depressed, agoraphobic, alcoholic, weighed over 300 pounds, and was trapped in an unhappy marriage. She refused to go for psychiatric help or even to see a physician or dentist despite her needs for such services. When her mother and two daughters spoke to her about at least seeing a doctor, she became enraged, so much so that her family became frightened and backed off. Laura died in an accident, after which her mother made a serious suicide attempt.

Many of Laura's relatives recognized there was a problem and that her behavior was self-destructive, but they felt helpless. That is why recognition and knowledge of how to respond is everybody's business. Telephone hot lines, suicide prevention centers, hospital emergency rooms, and similar organizations should be available to a much larger body of people.

It is especially the traditional gatekeepers and health professionals who have to know the danger signs and response procedures. These include doctors, social workers, psychologists, rehabilitation and guidance counselors, police, firemen, clergy, and possibly even bartenders.

Because of the nature of their work, nurses, activities therapists, and occupational therapists are confronted with many seriously suicidal persons. As Pronsati (1990) pointed out, "Occupational therapists are often the health professionals who first witness symptoms of depression."

Doctors are especially important because the majority of elderly people who commit suicide have seen a physician within a month of their fatal act. The family physician is a particularly important and potentially life saving figure (Sanborn, Niswander, & Casey, 1970). Psychological autopsies and other epidemiological studies indicate that the bulk of these suicides suffered from a treatable depression (Conwell, 1991). Too often, however, the doctor does not recognize the danger signs, does not inquire, and when he or she does, the inquiry is insufficient. That may even be true of psychiatrists.

> Gertrude P. was a 75-year-old woman who was taken to see a psychiatrist by her son, to whom she had confided feeling very depressed and suicidal. The psychiatrist interviewed Mrs. P., who admitted she was suicidal, but added that she would never kill herself because of the damage it would cause to her family. The doctor prescribed some medication and advised her to apply at the local mental hygiene clinic. Mrs. P. accepted the medication and two days later committed suicide.

The psychiatrist had not interviewed Mrs. P.'s son individually, and had not explored her past history of psychiatric treatment. He was not aware of a long history of breakdowns and hospitalizations. It is surprising yet tragically frequent that despite this history, she had never been seen in continuous therapy by one person. Had the doctor conducted a systematic, thorough assessment, as described in this chapter, the suicide might have been prevented.

As Mrs. P.'s case illustrates, the external situation and experience of the suicidal person includes the doctor or therapist. Therefore, an important danger sign is the ignorance of the examiner about both the indicators of suicidal risk and the nature of the aging process. Ignorance is particularly ominous when compounded by bias or ageism. A major depression is often masked as somatic complaints. That is why the reported symptoms of an elderly person should never be dismissed and ridiculed. Yet, it is all to frequent for a depressed person to be prescribed a lethal dose of sleeping pills or other medications, even when the patient tells the physician that he is suicidal (Haggerty, 1973).

Watts (1961) described cases where danger signs of suicide were present but had been ignored or minimized by the doctor. With a more comprehensive viewpoint than many physicians, he advocated that the doctor must not only recognize the symptoms of danger signs of suicide, he "Must be approachable and easy of access to the patient." Dr. Watts went on to say that the doctor should also be approachable to the relatives. "After all, the family unit is the first line of defense and if only relatives can learn to discuss their worry about a husband or wife who has swung into a depressive mood, then perhaps we shall be able to get down to early treatment and so lower the suicide rate" (1961, p. 265).

Because the doctor is such a potential suicide prevention force, the physician's role is considered in more detail in later chapters. Suffice it to emphasize here that every physician has to become familiar, not only with the recognition signs, but how to respond to them. Many physicians do not inquire about suicide because they would not know what to do if a patient were to acknowledge such feelings.

The inadequate professional preparation of some doctors may extend to their misunderstanding of complaints by almost all the elderly.

Martha B. complained of stomach pains for many months while her physician patiently explained that women are prone to psychosomatic symptoms as they get older. He came increasingly irritated and finally agreed to a upper GI series in order to shut her up. He was very chagrined when the examination disclosed a serious stomach ulcer.

This book assumes that the reader is more humanistic and open-minded.

The recognition of a suicidal risk is not enough; there must be communication to those involved. Recognition without communication can lead to a serious suicidal act. One 19-year-old man told his father he wanted to kill himself. His father did not notify anyone of this conversation until after his son committed suicide (Richman, 1986).

Such failures in communication can happen with professionals as well. One woman brought her 21-year-old brother to a psychiatric emergency room because he said he was suicidal. The resident who examined him sent him home, even though the relatives said they felt uncomfortable about his condition. That night he killed himself. The patient had told the resident of his suicidal state, and described the plan he had devised. The resident did not tell the relatives, in the belief that what the patient told him was confidential and therefore privileged information.

Such naive behavior could be understood because the resident had just begun his training. It could be considered a criticism of the training situation in psychiatry where the most seriously disturbed patients, the ones who come to the emergency room, are seen by those who are least experienced. Actually, the resident could have protected the confidentially by calling in the relatives and having the young man tell them himself.

Once the possibility of a suicidal state is recognizes, the evaluation proceeds from there, covering all the major components associated with suicidal despair. With the individual and family risk factors described in Chapter 1 as a base, the evaluation adds the degree of decompensation of defenses and coping devices, whether individuation and a sense of self are present, whether the integrity of the self is seriously threatened, and whether social and family supports and resources are available.

A quantitative assessment of suicidal risk can be made by using the information in the previous chapter. Table 1.1 on the recognition signs, and Table 5.1, on the family at the time of a suicidal state, combine into a valuable checklist of suicidal potential. The more such signs in the suicidal person, as well as the family and social networks, the greater the risk. The procedure is illustrated in the following example.

> Jack B., a 75-year-old man, was referred for outpatient treatment after 2 years of hospitalization at a psychiatric facility following the death of his wife in a suicide pact. He killed his wife, then attempted suicide and almost succeeded.
>
> Mr. B. arrived on time for our session. A medium sized, tense looking, tight lipped man, he walked with a limp, and held a paralyzed right arm close to his body. The disabilities were the result of his failed suicide act. He was uncommunicative and seemed hostile during the therapy sessions. He declared that he did not believe in psychotherapy and that he only agreed to treatment in order to be discharged from the hospital. He resisted disclosing any personal information, and in particular refused to talk about the events and details leading up to the suicidal episode. Nevertheless, he freely expressed remorse at what happened and the belief that both he and his wife were mentally ill at the time. He said that he was sorry that he did not die with his wife, and that he wished he were dead now. However, he denied being suicidal.

How would you rate this gentleman? Tables 1.1 and 5.1 provide a usable measure. Each category was rated as low, moderate, or severe, utilizing the headings from I to V on Table 1.1, and the family characteristics on Table 5.1. The following ratings were made.

I. Ego-weakening factors.

The rating was low. He does not have a major physical illness, does not drink, and is not in intractable pain. He does have a diagnosis of major depression in remission, with residues. In addition, his frustration tolerance was low, he could withstand very little stress, and he quickly became angry. He was resistant to treatment, but on the other hand, has never missed an appointment and has always been on time, or early.

II.   Social isolation factors.

The rating is of low to moderate social isolation. The patient moved from the sheltered and structured setting of a mental hospital to the sheltered, structured but freer setting of an Adult Home. He maintains very superficial relationships with the other residents, eating and watching television together and engaging in occasional conversations about weather and current events. However, the move brought him physically closer to his family.

III.   Dynamic and situational factors.

The rating is moderate with some danger signs. The patient did attempt suicide previously, and lost his wife in a most grievous and traumatic manner. Aside from the loss of his wife, he had retired from his work with suggestions of feelings of failure and being unwanted. Problems with peers are potentially present. He directly acknowledges that he avoids intimate contact because of the possible conflicts that would emerge. Dependency is not a problem, but apathy definitely is. There were several recent crises in the lives of his children, which had the effect of moving them further away from him emotionally. The overall impression is of vulnerability to suicidal risk, which is not at present high.

IV.   Attitudinal and communication factors.

The rating is again moderate. Jack B. rejects help on one level, yet even in our silent meetings I feel an unspoken appeal from him. He is definitely uncommunicative, and resorts to much denial; however, his communications are not indirect or double binding. He is irritable, does not feel hopeful, but on the other hand is not in a state of despair, nor does he believe that he is a burden. There are no direct or indirect expressions of suicidal plans or impulses.

His children are very angry at him and very blaming and they rarely come to visit. On the other hand, they went out of their way to arrange for him to be discharged from the hospital and placed nearer their home. He is invited to all the major holidays and other family events.

V.   Recovery factors.

There was so much varied material in this category that any one rating was all but impossible. Although subject to change, the rating is of a moderate amount of recovery factors for suicide, but low in capacities for a rich and satisfying life.

On the negative side, the patient possesses only a minimal capacity for empathy and interpersonal relatedness. There is a dearth of wisdom. He has learned from experience mainly to avoid potentially hurtful situations, something like a wounded animal who has retreated to a cave. Consequently, there is little in the way of active coping skills.

On the positive side, he does exhibit a sense of humor. He maintains an interest in current affairs and enjoys passive activities such as watching television. Because of the structure of the adult home in which he lives, watching television takes place in a group or social setting. As for external recovery factors, his family can be rated as ambivalent, but in a true emergency, they are available. Similarly, his therapist is interested, caring, and available, although frequently exasperated.

Remember, this is the rating of Jack B.'s current state. From all indications, the ratings at the time of his tragic suicidal act would have been high in the risk factors, and low in the recovery factors. In addition these ratings must be considered in the context of Table 5.1, the family characteristics. These are divided into seven major divisions, from Separation Intolerance to Crisis Intolerance. While these have been summarized in the previous chapter, the Family Therapy Chapter contains a fuller background and rationale. Jack B.'s family ratings were as follows.

I. An inability to accept necessary change.

Jack B. scores very high. He cannot tolerate separation; his relationships are symbiotic; he keeps early relationships alive by not sharing them with anyone else; and he does not mourn, except in the deepest recesses of his private life.

II. Role demands and interpersonal conflicts.

At this point in time, Mr. B. is rated as low to moderate, primarily because he has given up his strivings and avoided meeting age appropriate role demands. This avoidance enables him to survive, but at the price of impoverishment.

III. A disturbed family structure.

Currently the rating is moderate. It is protected from becoming higher because everyone in the family is keeping their distance, fortunately without outright rejection or abandonment. Were they to do so, the suicide risk rating would increase dramatically.

IV. *Disturbed intrafamily relationships.*

The rating is moderate. A family interview indicated that there were severe unresolved resentments and disturbances in his intrafamily relationships, which are also being avoided by both the relatives and by Mr. B.

V. *Affective difficulties.*

The rating is similar to the above; moderate because of avoidance. Otherwise the rating would be high, with elevated suicidal risk.

VI. *Communicative disturbances.*

The rating is moderate; while the potential for suicidal risk is high.

VII. *An intolerance for crises.*

The rating for current crisis difficulties is low. The rating for an intolerance for crises of separation, should they appear, is very high, with a high risk of suicide.

Comment.   The above checklist suggests that at the present time, Jack B. is at low-to-moderate risk for suicide, despite the traumatic history of a suicide pact. However, his success, if it may be called that, is achieved by an extreme use of avoidance, apathy, denial, superficiality, and the atrophy of his abilities.

With the family ratings there is evidence of many unfinished problems and conflicts and much ambivalence. However, ambivalence is not a purely negative term. It means that where hate is present, there is also love. Should his children become involved in a major crisis, they may reject, abandon, and scapegoat Jack B. and he would then become a very high risk for suicide.

A comparison of Tables 1.1 and 5.1 indicates a fundamental relationship between them. High ratings on Table 1.1 are primarily related to the vulnerability of the individual to suicide. High ratings on Table 5.1 are based upon a sensitivity to external sources of stress, especially those involving the family or family-like relationships. Table 5.1, therefore, presents the situational conditions, or the family context that potentiate a suicidal state in someone who is vulnerable.

Many of the family characteristics are highly volatile, vulnerable to anxiety and developmental demands, and subject to change. Their unpredictability not only reflects a danger, especially when not explored further by the examiner, but on the positive side is related to the fortunately large number of vulnerable suicidal elderly who continue to live and sometimes even thrive.

The internal state and situational context of the suicidal person at the time of a seriously suicidal state can be summed up as "The Exhaustion Factor." This includes four major parameters: The exhaustion of the individual and his or her ability to cope or functional; the exhaustion of the resources of the family and other significant persons so they are not able to help and may even be at risk themselves; the presence of a crisis which is perceived by everyone as insoluble; and finally, the acceptance of suicide as the solution.

The burden theme is a major component of the exhaustion factor. A review of cases in which the suicidal person reports the feeling of being a burden, and of relatives who feel they are burdened leads to the definition of the term, which recognizes the context. The terms "being a burden," or "feeling burdened" refer to an interactional situation characterized by a high degree of stress. The result is symptom formation in the relatives or significant others, including unusual symptomatic behaviors, such as sudden marital infidelity, and an intractable quality to the symptoms of the patient.

Being a burden, therefore, can best be understood as part of a family or social network in trouble, where the usual coping mechanisms are not working, but the status quo can not continue and a major change is required. The symptomatic behavior in both the patient and the other family members can be seen as a way of preventing a change in the relationship except by the ill person becoming expendable. That is when suicide and euthanasia are seen as solutions.

It is evident that being or feeling burdened cannot be viewed as an individual matter. It always implies the involvement of others, with the burden being a response to a *system* under stress. Similar reflections may also apply to stressed and overly burdened house physicians when faced by patients in need of special physical care, especially when called in the middle of the night after 36 hours of continuous duty.

Exhaustion of resources associated with suicide thus includes a state of pervasive despair, failure, and hopelessness in the suicidal person, the family system, and the social network. The problem or crisis that is perceived as intolerable yet insoluble is combined with a compulsion to take some action to resolve the tension. In the accurate assessment of the suicidal elderly, the problem is that stressful life events comprise the typical fate of elderly people. Although old age is a time of loss, illness, decline, and social rejection, most of the elderly respond in an affirmative, or at least nonsuicidal, manner.

In other words, there may be many false positives. That has been a problem for many investigators in their efforts to predict those who are likely to commit suicide. Many people whose ratings indicate a high suicide risk do not kill themselves. In my experience the majority of those who test at a high risk are genuinely so.

Since suicide is such a complex, multidetermined condition, it is unrealistic to think that any one test or evaluation could be an effective diagnostic indicator of risk. It is also unrealistic to predict a future act that is so dependent upon a present situation that does not enter into the assessment.

Most of all it is not only unrealistic but almost cruel to neglect the ones who test high on measures of lethality but who have rejected suicide. Taking into account the suffering, despair, and many other blows to the self and loved ones, they too are entitled to treatment and stress reduction.

It follows that "false positives" are not messages to be corrected or disregarded, but communications or warning flags that help is needed. Others who are high in risk factors may have the resources or the family and social supports needed to overcome their despair. Most suicide risk assessment instruments do not explore the family and environmental features, which so often make the difference between life and death.

The other "problem" is that the purpose of predicting suicide is preventing suicide. In other words, a prediction of suicide is made, which then initiates measures to make the prediction false, such as hospitalization when necessary, medication and other physical measures, and psychotherapy. Such false positives are wonderful, and to be encouraged. In addition, survival is a tribute to the strengths of old people. The difference between life and death, as we have noted, requires the acceptance of suicide, and most of the elderly, even those in despair, value life too much to end it.

ASSESSMENT AND TESTING

Psychological testing must be adapted to the elderly person. Suicide is so situationally determined and has so much to do with the role of others that individual psychological testing omits too many of the pertinent variables.

Testing does have its place, as long as it's adapted to the client and the reasons for referral. However, most of the time-consuming tests of intelligence and personality were not devised for the elderly and their life tasks. Intelligence tests were mainly devised for people in school, the armed forces, and the work force. In addition, there is an excessive emphasis in the literature on the assessment of the elderly upon mental decline and senility. These must be assessed, but not at the expense of evaluating the assets and areas of competence of the individual.

Much more valuable is the approach of Jerome Fisher (1973), who reported on the basis of a series of studies that social competence, effectiveness, and likability, combined with social and cognitive accessibility were more valid concepts for evaluating the elderly than a focus upon intellectual impairment. I find that Fisher's emphasis upon social skills and their applications can serve as an operational measure of Durkheim's social integration, while his concepts of social and cognitive accessibility touch significantly upon ego functioning and the capacity to relate to others.

I last spoke to David Wechsler, the author of the Wechsler Intelligence Scales, a few months before he died at the age of 85. His mind was still active, preoccupied at the time with developing the "Wechsler Intelligence Scale for the Elderly," or WISE. Unfortunately he was not able to work on this project. However, the contributions of Fisher, Zigler, and others, may develop into the eventual constriction of the WISE.

Figure Drawings have been a helpful resource for evaluation in the context of diagnostic and family interviews. It is a particularly valuable procedure as a screening device for suicidal potential, in the context of a diagnostic or therapeutic interview. (See Richman, 1986, pp. 86–105, for a more detailed description of the Figure Drawing analysis.)

Figure Drawings, combined with a brief mental status examination, the Bender-Gestalt, and the brief Rorschach procedure described by Klopfer (1984), are very useful as an effective yet relatively brief psychological screening battery for suicidal potential. This battery is extremely informative, covering many areas, including the presence of suicidal thoughts or impulses and other danger signs, as well as resources for recovery. To further assess the crisis and problem areas which may be precipitating the suicidal state, a family oriented crisis inventory is recommended, such as the Index of Family Tensions (Wells & Rabiner, 1973).

There is one omission in the statistics. In my experience, there is a high rate of suicidal *Ideation* in the depressed or emotionally disturbed elderly. That offers a valuable clinical lead when interviewing for the purpose of determining suicidal intent. By and large, suicide is the culmination of a process which begins with a cognitive event—the thought of suicide—and ends with an irrevocable act. An inspection of Table 1.1 illustrates the prominence of suicidal ideation in the clinical recognition signs.

Finally, the feedback of test results has provided very meaningful information (Richman, 1967). Dr. Ida Davidoff and I found that interaction testing of couples in a marital crisis, followed by feedback of the findings to the couples, was a therapeutic experience for many of those involved (Richman & Davidoff, 1971). The examiner also obtains further information from other professional sources including physicians and social workers who have had contact with the patient, ward and hospital records, and previous diagnostic evaluations.

THE ASSESSMENT AND CRISIS INTERVENTION INTERVIEW

The specific assessment procedures are essentially the same at all ages, as described in several of my previous publications (Richman, 1984, 1986, 1991; Richman & Eyman, 1990). Basically, the steps consist of an organized series of brief individual interviews with the suicidal person and relatives, followed by a family session in which each member of the family is initially seen alone.

In my work the family interview has been the most crucial procedure in the entire diagnostic process. It has led to the formation of a workable treatment plan, the determination of dispositions, such as whether or not to hospitalize, and has been the beginning of rapport and a therapeutic alliance. Effective diagnostic interviewing is simultaneously good therapy.

When a suicidal person is referred for treatment, I have the family come in, as many members as possible. If an elderly client is referred or is seen in the hospital or clinic with a spouse, I obtain permission to use the telephone to call in children and other members of the family. It is usually more effective and therapeutic for the therapist to phone and establish some contact than to leave it to the patient. That is also a message to the family about how seriously the therapist regards the situation.

Many depressed and suicidal elderly persons refuse permission for their children to appear, in the belief that they are protecting their offspring. There are also hints of fears that they will lose power and control over whatever fading autonomy they still possess. In some cases there is a sensitivity to a perceived stigma, and they want to keep their help-seeking a secret. Eventually, the majority do agree to a family session, and the results are invariably positive. I accept and am appreciative of whoever does appear. Inexperienced therapists may need guidance and support in these procedures.

> One therapist asked a suicidal patient to arrange a family interview. The result was that only two relatives agreed to appear and the patient reported that her husband said he would not attend a meeting with them. After consultation with a supervisor, and with the patient's permission, the therapist called the husband. He was cooperative, and had no objection to relatives being at the session and offered to invite others. For this particular diagnostic session, 11 family members attended, and all participated actively.

When I first meet the family in the waiting room, I introduce myself and state that we will be getting together for the purpose of furthering harmonious family relationships. First, however, I want to see each person individually.

The individual meetings are brief, unless the person has a great need to talk to ventilate, which they are permitted to do. I ask their perception of the situation, and accept whatever they say. Then I obtain Figure Drawings from each person, thank them for their cooperation, and invite them to collaborate with me in the therapeutic endeavor.

In terms of information and establishing rapport, the individual contacts provide a nonstressful preparation for the family interview. The therapist obtains a sense of the family as both individuals and an organization; the participants obtain a sense of the therapist as both an individual and a professional. The family often thinks the interviewer knows everything by the time the family meeting rolls around.

Three major recommendations for the family interview include the following. First, a positive, accepting, and approving reaction to the turmoil and expressions of stress is most salutary. Second, the participants in the therapy encounter are commended for being such good patients by letting it all out, and they are encouraged to continue their intense interaction. Third is the use of various interventions, such as relabeling. Expressions of overt death wishes, for example, such as "Why don't you kill yourself; we can't stand it the way you are; you're making mother sick and killing her," are relabeled as expressions of complete exasperation and of not knowing how to deal with the situation.

The basic procedures of the assessment interview, the monitoring or depression, death wishes, exhaustion of resources, and the ability to respond to the therapeutic process, are presented in further detail in Chapter 4, on "The Healing Process."

On the basis of all the information obtained and on the evaluation, an initial treatment plan is drawn up, including goals, objectives, target symptoms or areas of intervention, and a disposition. Many of the patients and families continued in treatment with the initial interviewer. Some were referred to another therapist, a clinic, or some other facility, and some were hospitalized.

All else being equal, I prefer to see my clients on an outpatient basis. However, hospitalization would be recommended given the following three conditions: the patient scores high as a serious risk on the recognition and family tables; the clinical assessment interviews suggest a high risk; family or other support systems are weak, unavailable, or exhausted.

My patients are seen for treatment of a suicidal state for a period of time extending from one session to 10 years. Many of the patients "dropped out" after one to five sessions. I realize now that the majority of these had been helped as a result of brief crisis intervention, combined with their own resources for recovery. Much of the treatment correspond to what de Shazar (1988), calls "solution oriented therapy," even though I did not think of the treatment in those terms. But I was also practicing crisis intervention before I had ever heard of the term.

In the succeeding quarter of a century or more since embarking on the adventure or understanding and helping the suicidal, I have become increasingly aware of the crisis aspects of suicide and the tremendous value of crisis intervention. The following chapter describes the nature of crisis intervention for elderly people at the time of a suicidal state, including the use of the constructive forces within suicidal persons and their support systems.

3

Crisis Intervention

A suicidal crisis is both a danger and an opportunity. I cannot sufficiently emphasize the importance of timing, of a therapist being there at the height of the emergency, someone whose intervention is accompanied by interest, understanding, and caring, together with the provision of measures that relieve anxiety and inspire hope.

Frank Pittman, Kal Flomenhaft, and the other therapists on the treatment team that successfully applied family crisis intervention as an alternative to hospitalization (Langsley, Kaplan et al., 1968) demonstrated how these measures can be applied to a wide variety of psychiatric disturbances. Their work will be discussed later in this chapter. My review of their cases suggested that over 40 percent of the patients they treated presented with suicidal or other self-destructive features.

The crisis in suicide involves a change—which can be biological, individual, or social, and most often some combination of these three—which is perceived as a threat to the entire family and social network system. A new development is required, usually of a tripartite nature, calling for a change in one's self-concept, interpersonal relationships, and social role. All of these imply concomitant changes in the family members and others.

Herman C., at age 76, was crushed when his wife died. He told his daughter that he saw no reason to live and wanted to kill himself. His daughter took him to the psychogeriatric clinic of Jacobi Hospital, where they were seen for one session. Mr. C. and his daughter had discussed their situation in the one day prior to their appointment. He had decided that with the help of his family he would go on living and make the best of his situation. During the session, they both grieved together and agreed that no further intervention was necessary.

The key factor in Mr. C.'s situation was the recognition that his family cared and that there was a support system available to see him through his bereavement and to share his grief. I have seen serious and even fatal suicidal acts precipitated by the false belief that no one cared. This one session, preceded by the decision to do something positive, was sufficient.

An individual in crisis is someone "who develops a sudden or rapid disorganization in his capacity to control his behavior or to carry out his usual personal, vocational and social activities." (Coleman & Errera, 1963; Coleman & Zwerling, 1959). The definition refers to behavior rather than any particular illness. It also refers to a universal condition, for everyone is confronted with crises, even therapists. How these crises are resolved determines the success or failure of growth and development.

Most suicidal acts are precipitated by crises that appear insoluble to the people involved, but these situations pose a promise of growth as well as a danger of destruction. Therefore, the positive aspects of crises need to become more well known. All effective treatment of suicide begins with crises intervention, which can propel those involved on the road to health.

The vital importance of crises and the need for immediate intervention was recognized some 50 years ago by Lindemann (1944) after a tragic fire at the Coconut Grove nightclub in Boston in 1940. Lindemann found that survivors who had lost loved ones did not recover physically until they were able to grieve emotionally for the loss.

Farberow (1967) described the crisis in suicide as a turning point that can be recognized by its quality of urgency and immediacy. A "turning point" is a valuable concept because it emphasizes how much a crisis is both an opportunity and a danger, depending upon how the turning takes place. The urgency of the situation is to be emphasized. People in a crisis are unable to wait; some form of action has to be taken at once. The usual defense mechanisms are no longer working. The resources of both the potentially suicidal person and his family and social network have become drained.

The present crisis is built upon past unresolved crises. If the crisis becomes one more unresolved situation, the outcome in those who are vulnerable may be either a completed suicide or the continuation of more destructive crisis events. If the crises is resolved positively, hopefully with the increased availability of creative and more effective coping skills, the effect may reverberate deep down into the ultimate successful resolution of past crises.

The effect of crisis intervention has been compared to pushing someone standing on one leg (Caplan, 1964). A relatively brief intervention can have profound beneficial effects. What actually happens depends upon how the crisis is met by the individual, the family system, and the social and other support networks, not simply by the individual alone. Crisis intervention cannot always be brief, and is not always sufficient.

Irene D. was in a state of deep depression and unexpressed grief following the death of her husband when she was 68. Her suicide note and overdose of sleeping pills, which would have been fatal except that she was only accidentally found, shocked her three children into a desire to examine their lives and relationships. She was hospitalized and discharged after 3 weeks, into my care.

Mrs. D. continued to be in a crisis state, depressed and dysfunctional for another month. Then, although no longer clinically depressed or suicidal, she and her family continued in psychotherapy, consisting of medication and a combination of family and individual sessions. Now, in her second year of treatment, she is coming to terms with her loneliness and losses, and building a life for herself, with the support and warm relationships with her family.

Although the process and procedures may differ depending on the needs of those involved, crisis intervention is always a beginning, often a rebirth, and therefore a reparation for loss. Suicidal crises in the elderly almost invariably involve such losses, which are experienced as irreparable, combined with an intolerance for the grief process. Crisis intervention relieves the anxiety and depression over separation, thus permitting a richer and more meaningful existence for whatever time is remaining. The positive effects continue, sometimes for years after a brief intervention.

AN OUTLINE OF CRISIS INTERVENTION

The emphasis is upon the here-and-now. The rule is to first deal with the immediate crisis, rather than to prematurely expand the therapeutic investigation in order to obtain a more complete picture, or to probe into the dynamic roots of the suicidal state.

There are six basic steps in crisis intervention: (1) establishing rapport; (2) pinpointing the crisis; (3) determining the degree of suicidal risk; (4) planning the intervention; (5) initiating the treatment procedures; and

(6) follow-up. (These are described further in earlier works, e.g., Richman, 1986.)

While details may change depending upon the nature of the case and the individual qualities of the situation and participants, the process is basically the same in all cases. Crisis intervention is one part of a total approach, which is typically multidisciplinary in nature. Most of the therapy with the suicidal elderly described in the chapters that follow, on the individual, group, and family psychotherapies, began with crisis intervention. Treatment is not usually sought unless there is a crisis.

The initial goal is the resolution of the major current crisis. However, the suicidal state does not usually arise de novo out of one crucial event. Erikson's formulation of development stages and their associated crises, combined with a family systems orientation, forms a valuable theoretical base for understanding the relationship between the historical roots and the here-and-now situation on which the crisis intervention is based.

What actually happens depends upon how the crisis is met by the individual, the family system, and the social and other support networks, not simply by the individual alone. A ripple effect is frequently observed.

Jenny E. attempted suicide after her mother died 20 years before. Now that she turned 80, her husband died, and she attempted suicide again. Her 50-year-old daughter then became depressed and phobic after her own husband suddenly died. At this point Mrs. E.'s 17-year-old grandson also attempted suicide.

The crisis in suicide involves a change that is perceived as threatening to the entire family and social network system. The necessary change in someone suffering a major loss implies concomitant changes in other family members. Otherwise, as in the family of Jenny E., there is a disruption of functioning and a spreading of self-destructive reactions.

A crisis bears some resemblance to the concept of trauma in its tendency to overwhelm the ego and coping resources of the person and family system, thus leaving the entire network vulnerable and helpless. The newer concept of posttraumatic stress disorder (PTSD) is similar and perhaps more comprehensive in emphasizing the broad biopsychosocial ramifications and potentially enduring effects of a crisis. PTSD is an idea associated with the Vietnam War, but it owes a great deal to the work of Hans Selye (1975).

In the literature on the development of the elderly, loss has acquired an expanded meaning beyond separation from others. It now includes the effect of retirement, and losses related to income, self-esteem, and health, which are hazardous situations and the basis for crises in general. However, they do not lead to suicide unless combined with the actual or threatened loss or separation from a significant person or persons. In contrast, the loss of an other, an actual person, especially when the relationship had been a symbiotic one, can by itself become the basis for suicide.

In other words, the *suicidal* crisis includes an actual or threatened separation from people. As a rule I never use the word "always" because in human events nothing can be counted on to happen always. Nevertheless, as I look through 25 years of clinical notes on suicidal people, there has always been a loss or separation involving others.

There are times when a nonfatal suicide attempt takes place in the context of severely stressful relationships where there is a threat of separation, followed by a more lethal act when the separation becomes permanent.

Fernando, M., a 70-year-old man, that attempted suicide after a forced retirement that led to increased marital dissension. That crisis was resolved, but when his wife died 10 years later, he completed the act and killed himself. Perhaps a recognition of the crisis and proper intervention could have prevented this later tragedy (reported in Richman, 1986).

The patient was hospitalized following his first attempt, but did not continue in treatment upon his discharge. I had evaluated him on the ward, and had no further contact, but remember him as a very kind, gentle man. It was by chance that I read about his completed suicide in a local paper.

Although not necessarily reported in the papers, such events are frequent. That is why one of the major recognition signs of suicidal potential is suicidal behavior in the past. The message is that crisis intervention is the treatment of choice in the first suicidal situation, as in all of them, but crisis intervention may not be enough. Follow-up contacts and interviews are essential.

As already noted (Richman, 1975) there are age differences in the nature of the crises that precipitate a suicidal act. Examples range from the threat of separation resulting from a child or an adolescent's increasing involvement with friends and activities outside the home, to its opposite—the threat of closeness and unaccustomed intimacy resulting from an older person's retirement. Or, to go full circle, the threat of separation and loss, based upon physical illness and ultimately, death.

A perennial question is, "Why now? Why on this particular day and moment?" Timing and the question of which day, or even which hour the act occurs, can determine the differences between life and death. Sheer accident sometimes plays a fateful role.

For example, there is evidence that Marilyn Monroe tried to obtain help during her final suicide attempt. She called her psychiatrist but he was away, as was her housekeeper, while her boyfriend would not or could not respond to her call (Guiles, 1969).

Such experiences have led to a number of practical recommendations. For examples, Mintz (1966) presents a number of practical safeguards including the removal of firearms and lethal medications from the home and careful monitoring of prescription drugs. Aside from the lifesaving nature of these measures, which of course is primary, they communicate the caring of the doctor and the family, and therefore the message that other people want the patient to live. Mintz also presents "quick symptomatic relief" as the goal, which corresponds to my emphasis upon early stress reduction through reducing separation anxiety and restoring family cohesion.

THE EFFECT OF PAST CRISES

The current crisis rests upon a foundation of past crises, each one determining growth and future development, with a cumulative impact on the current situation. Development proceeds through a series of crises, each one influencing future developments. How these early crises were met is critical to how the current one is handled. In therapy, however, these earlier aspects are kept in abeyance until the current crisis is resolved.

The suicidal crisis involves loss and separation because the basic conflicts and dynamics of the suicidal person and family are rooted in early relationships and past experiences of separation. As a result, unresolved crises from the past carry more weight than we generally realize.

When she was 5 years old, Karen F. was subjected to threats of drastic punishment by her father if she did not behave. Shortly after, father left home and mother obtained a divorce. Father then committed suicide. The little girl loved her father and felt she was to blame for his departure and death.

When she grew up, she married, then divorced, after which her ex-husband also committed suicide. She was very attached to him and never resolved the loss. She remarried, an attachment which was very close and at least at times a happy one. However, she suffered from periodic depressive breakdowns.

One day she was in great emotional pain and despair, and her husband was similarly depressed. They agreed upon a suicide pact. Her husband killed her using, at her request, the actual drastic punishment threatened by her father 70 years earlier.

The stress and need for completion that could not be met because of the loss of her father 70 years ago could be seen as the basic crisis in Karen F.'s life upon which other crises were built. It is as though an unresolved crisis forms a nucleus, like a grain of sand from which an oyster grows a pearl, but it is a very deadly object that grows.

The strength and tenacity of early bonds and the desperate, life-threatening reactions when they are broken, help explain how unresolved crises from the past maintain early maladaptive life patterns. It is as though they became unfinished tasks whose influence would not go away.

In a series of studies, Elsa Zeigarnik (Ellis, 1938) found that people remembered unfinished tasks more than finished ones. Work with suicidal patients and their families suggests that something similar is true of crises. While unfinished crises may not necessarily be remembered more, they *are* acted out and repeated more than finished or resolved ones. Therefore, the question is not only *how* past crises were resolved, but *if* they were resolved.

Such reflections lead to the hypothesis that there is a basic crisis in chronically disturbed or suicidogenic families, a crisis which is repeated, sometimes from generation to generation, until it is resolved. One reason for maintaining a rigid status quo is that this unreconciled past has become incorporated into the present. Consequently, to change the status quo means to lose the relationship with the early loved ones in the primary family.

These early disturbances are often related to inadequate or insufficient mothering, leading to a craving to be cared for and loved unconditionally. Carl Whitaker (Neill & Kniskern, 1982) and other therapists have discussed the importance of the therapist as a mother figure regardless of the sex of the therapist, for severely disturbed patients of those who were emotionally deprived at an early age. In the family of the suicidal, this craving for an all-loving mother is handed down from one generation to the other.

One major finding in my investigations is that the parents of suicidal persons had suffered even more early losses than the suicidal person herself or himself. I suspect that is why a nurturing quality in the therapist is important, in order to make contact with these basic early needs and relationships, not only in the suicidal person but in the entire family.

These reflections on parenting in general and mothering in particular touch upon the essence of the origins of suicide and its treatment. They are discussed further in the context of transference and counter transference in Chapter 4, which follows.

PSYCHOTHERAPY AND THE THERAPEUTIC CRISIS

Crises are present before the suicidal crisis that brings the person into treatment, and they continue after the initial crisis is resolved and the person or family is in therapy. The negative therapeutic reaction is the most well-known example of a crisis during therapy. However, there is much evidence that almost all progress in the treatment of the suicidal condition proceeds through a series of crises. That is true whether the patient is treated in the office or hospital, in individual treatment, in family therapy, or in group therapy.

Crises are an intrinsic part of life and growth, without which no progress can take place. They occur when one is faced with disaster, but they also accompany the sometimes fearful prospect of recovery and health.

Boss (1963) described such a crisis in one very disturbed schizophrenic woman who was beginning to give up her psychotic symptoms and way of life. The patient called one night and screamed into the phone, "I want to rip my belly open with a big carving knife! I want to slash my arteries and suck my own blood! Just thinking about it makes my mouth water." The therapist hurried to her immediately.

He found her in a psychotic and disorganized state. "How could anyone get better," the therapist asked reassuringly, "without the old neurotic world collapsing in the process?... Suicide is always only a mistake in seizing the wrong medium. You feel compelled to effect a physical cutting open of your body. You have an urge to see your actual blood run because you don't dare, as yet, to open your heart and let your feeling flow. You don't even trust yourself far enough to admit to either one of us that you like me because I try to stand by you" (1963, p. 20).

These interventions led to a tremendous lessening of tension and of her psychotic state. A reassuring discussion of her dependency needs followed. Dr. Boss's availability, even late at night, was a vital part of his patient's recovery. Eventually she was evidently cured and became a successful physician and an accomplished artist.

In addition to availability, other curative influences in this case included Dr. Boss's empathy, humanism, acceptance of her whether ill or well, regressed or recovered, his realistically positive attitude, willingness to acknowledge that he had been mistaken in his understanding of her (that occurred at the beginning of therapy), and his willingness to see her through the therapeutic crises. These are the qualities universally found in the dedicated and committed psychotherapist of suicidal people.

Another quality is patience and the realization that difficult situations must be repeated and resolved over and over. To be with a patient is perhaps the most valuable form of healing reassurance, especially during the periodic crises and negative therapeutic reactions that are typical of nearly all suicidal patients.

"But it was to happen again dozens of times," Boss wrote, "that these two opposed phases—the state of the happy, symptom-free child and that of the tormented psychotic—alternated with and followed one another. The pathological phase could be predicted with empiric certainty each time the patient was confronted with the realm of her sensual and emotional grown-up femininity. [This variation between crisis and recovery] was fundamentally the only and indispensable therapeutic measure by which one could make accessible to her a genuine maturing, a slow assembling of all her life potentialities and their integration into a self-reliant, mature, and independent self. All that was needed was gradually to extend what one asked of her in the way of sustaining these exposures to the onslaught from areas of life native to phenomena of adult love" (1963, p. 23).

It would appear that effective psychotherapy with the suicidal person requires an intuitive and trained knowledge of the nature of crises and crisis intervention, and a firm commitment to seeing the patient through every one of these crises. Those not familiar with crisis intervention, the negative therapeutic reaction, the need to work with families and other social support systems, and the need never to give up on a patient, may eventually be resigned to, or even approving of suicide. A painfully contrasting approach to the one presented in this book was recommended by Bleuler, who coined the term, "schizophrenia." (1950, originally published 1908). He wrote:

In patients with an uncontrollable drive to inflict injury upon themselves, it is advisable to use a restraining sheet, which is more easily applied than the wet pack and which makes no pretense (recognized by the staff as well as by the patients) as constituting a medical measure ...if no results can be obtained by means of kindness and greatest possible indulgence, I believe that it is preferable to experiment with the use of restraint rather than to permit the patient to destroy himself (p. 485).

Could these patients be in a crisis, even if they are schizophrenic, and could their "uncontrollable drive to inflict injury upon themselves" be the expression of that crisis? I believe so. In those schizophrenics I have seen who are suicidal, their symptoms, including hallucinated voices and delusions, could also be fruitfully understood and treated as the expression of a crisis that needed resolution, not only as the incomprehensible symptom of disease. In the quote that follows, Dr. Bleuler recommends permitting schizophrenics to kill themselves, rather than forcing them to maintain an unendurable existence.

I fear that Dr. Bleuler did not possess the realistically positive attitude and willingness to see schizophrenic patients through therapeutic crises that typified Boss's approach, and that of John Rosen (1970). It is true that Bleuler lived and worked in a different era, with a fatalistic and negative attitude towards mental illness, and that he did not have access to the more recent psychotropic drugs, which help control psychotic symptoms and behavior. He was himself ambivalent about whether to prevent suicide in a severely suicidal person. It was Bleuler who brought to the world's attention the importance of ambivalence in schizophrenia. Perhaps he was also endowed with a generous portion of that quality; and suicide does tend to bring out ambivalence.

To his credit, Bleuler was opposed to a purely custodial, prison-like approach. As he said:

> The most serious of all schizophrenic symptoms is the suicidal drive. I am even taking this opportunity to state clearly that our present-day social system demands great, and entirely inappropriate cruelty from the psychiatrist in this respect. People are being forced to continue to live a life that has become unbearable for them for valid reasons; this alone is bad enough. However, it is even worse when life is made increasingly intolerable for these patients by using every means to subject them to constant humiliating surveillance. Most of our worst restraining measures would be unnecessary, if we were not duty-bound to preserve the patients' lives which, for them as well as for other, are only of negative value. (pp. 488–489)

Ellen West is the name given to a famous case of suicide by "free choice" (Binswanger, 1958). She was a chronically very suicidal woman who was in treatment with a psychoanalyst who was committed to working with her. However, her parents removed her from that therapy 0and had her admitted to a mental hospital in Switzerland where she was seen by Dr. Bleuler, who diagnosed her as an incurable schizophrenic. She was then sent home, even though "it was clear that a release from the institution meant certain suicide," (1958, p. 266) where she killed herself.

I wonder to what degree her family's opposition to her psychotherapy was based upon a negative therapeutic reaction. In a similar vein, to what degree was Dr. Bleuler's labeling of her as "incurable" based upon competition and opposition to psychotherapeutic treatment of schizophrenics—if that, in fact, was the correct diagnosis.

Therapists, including those as eminent and qualified as Dr. Bleuler or Dr. Freud, do not always know what they are doing, even though they think they do, and are frequently not aware of their own role in the situation. The error is compounded when the therapists then assume an air of righteousness and self-admiration, as did Binswanger and Bleuler, rather than recognizing their suicidogenic role.

CRISIS INTERVENTION AND HOSPITALIZATION

Langsley, Kaplan, and their coworkers (1968) demonstrated that family crisis intervention is as effective as hospitalization, and sometimes more so, in the treatment of psychiatric disorders. They organized a specially trained family crisis team, available on a 24-hour basis. I visited their unit in 1967, was very impressed with their work. The possibilities for an emergency-based crisis intervention team for inpatient services, and perhaps outpatient medical clinics, is discussed later in this chapter.

Nevertheless, hospitalization should not be blithely disregarded when treating suicidal people, especially the elderly. Hospitalization can be consistent with a crisis-oriented approach; it need not be lengthy. Langsley et al. (1968) occasionally kept a patient overnight in the emergency room in order to afford a temporary respite from stress and tension for the entire family. Henisz and Johnson (1977) and others (Rhine & Mayerson, 1971; Weisman, Feirstein & Thomas, 1969) integrated brief hospitalization with a crisis-oriented approach. They found that crisis hospitalization can be very effective for some patients, others may require longer term hospitalization, and still others may do better in outpatient treatment.

One consideration is the availability of qualified therapists to treat suicidal people on an outpatient basis.

> Seventy-four-year-old Allan S. hung himself one evening during a party in his home and was hospitalized on the medical service. The liaison psychiatrist who examined him made arrangements to transfer him to a psychiatric hospital. Mr. S.'s wife phoned me, requesting a second opinion, and I agreed to see him at his bedside. However, once the doctor was assured that a qualified therapist was interested and available, he discharged him home, to my therapeutic care.

Similar examples were frequent during my association with the hospital emergency room. For example it was not unusual for an emergency room doctor to call and ask, "Do you have room for another suicidal patient? If not, we will hospitalize him."

Properly handled, all of the options—outpatient crisis intervention, brief crisis hospitalization, and long term hospitalization—can be very therapeutic.

For some people, however, hospitalization is unacceptable to them, frequently because it implies having a dreaded mental disease. It is as though the demons thought to create madness in ancient times and that lurk in so many 19th Century novels and plays, such as in Ibsen's *Ghosts*, have never been exorcised. Such fears are still alive.

The terror of hospitalization may combine with the fact that it removes the suicidal person from the family and from ordinary pursuits of everyday life. The cure can then be worse than the disease. However, hospitalization can save lives.

> Seventy-three-year-old Ava G. came to the clinic with a 30-year history of bipolar disorder, with numerous episodes and hospitalizations. She was becoming increasingly depressed and agitated. Her 40-year-old son was marrying a woman who seemed to regard Mrs. G. as a bad influence and a threat to herself. Mrs. G. had responded well to hospitalization in the past but now she feared such an event would provide further ammunition that her new daughter-in-law would use to separate her from her son. She began developing quasi-delusional ideas that a yeast infection was the cause of all her problems. As her agitation increased, she nevertheless denied suicidal impulses. However, her Figure Drawings contained suicidal features.
>
> She held herself together until after the wedding. At the next therapy session she continued to deny suicidal impulses but her vague thoughts and allusions made me, as the therapist, very uncomfortable. I took her to the Psychiatric Emergency Room, and arranged for her to be admitted. She was angry at me but acknowledged to the admitting doctor that she had been planning to kill herself upon her return home.

Mrs. G. had refused all psychiatric medication and, in addition, her two children refused to appear for family sessions. In cases such as these, hospitalization is a welcome form of crisis intervention.

On the other hand, there are numerous cases that illustrate the deadly effects of hospitalization, cases either improperly handled or facing impossible resistance, sabotage of treatment, or other obstacles. Statistically there is no evidence that hospitalization prevents suicide. On the contrary, the greatest risk of suicide is found on admission to and discharge from hospitals. The danger is especially great, in my experience, when hospitalization is either disapproved of by the family and patient, or results in a further alienation of the patient from the family.

Like all other treatment measures, the therapist must be aware of the function of hospitalization to those involved, its meaning, perhaps distorted, to the patient and family, and the procedures by which hospitalization takes place. One of the features to be monitored is the attitude of the suicidal person and family to treatment in general, and hospitalization or medication in particular. Insights into these areas may be obtained particularly in artistic and literary figures. Many of the accounts of the suicides by such persons describe the opposition of the family to their hospitalizations (e.g., Swados, 1991; Middlebrook, 1991).

Ideally, hospitalization is a valuable form of crisis intervention and tension reduction, which can be the beginning of cure. The problem arises when hospitalization is imbued with the fears and conflict of the family, intertwined with a disturbance in the doctor/patient relationship, or disrupted by maladaptive attitudes of the patient, and sometimes the doctor.

For example, author William Styron described how he became seriously depressed and suicidal, with his condition not alleviated by his outpatient psychiatric treatment. Nevertheless, his doctor advised against hospitalization because of the stigma. Would you want a doctor who considered your treatment a stigma? No physician who holds such views should be treating people for emotional disturbances. Mr. Styron came within a hair's breadth of killing himself, but finally was hospitalized at his own insistence (Styron, 1990). In this case hospitalization was the most effective form of treatment. It allowed Styron a rest and temporary regression, both creating a needed respite from tension and despair.

As I have noted earlier (Richman, 1986, pp. 170–172) a permissive and accepted period of regression can be very therapeutic with severely depressed and suicidal people. In the case of the 28-year-old woman I call Ruth L. (p. 170), she became profoundly withdrawn, depressed, helpless, regressed, and unable to work, care for her apartment, or herself.

She refused to leave her bed, eat, or attend therapy sessions. Her mother moved in to take care of her and nurse her. Ruth L. was seen daily at home for therapy, with her mother participating in the sessions. Ruth recovered dramatically, and resumed her social life and her career with increasing success and satisfaction.

I have already referred to the remarkable treatment by Medard Boss (1963), of a suicidal and schizophrenic woman whom he encouraged to regress whenever her improvement and growth became too threatening to her. She recovered completely from both her suicidal and schizophrenic states.

In these last two examples, the therapeutic regression took place without hospitalization, but the right hospital setting can perform a similar function. However, such progress does not take place when the patient and family find the outpatient treatment or the inpatient hospitalization unacceptable.

Elizabeth Swados is an eminent playwright and composer, whose mother was hospitalized because of a massive depression with suicidal ideation. She responded well, her symptoms decreased, she displayed an increased interest in the outside world, and welcomed the opportunity to be cared for. However, her family reacted with fear and revulsion to the more blatantly psychotic patients on the ward. They also objected to the patient's "little girl" behavior. Eventually, her mother did commit suicide (Swados, 1991).

When a regression is not recognized as therapeutic it stops being therapeutic. The effects of treatment depend upon the perceptions of the patient and significant others. In suicidal states that depends upon effective treatment with the family.

THE PSYCHIATRIC EMERGENCY ROOM AND OTHER CRISIS CENTERS

The upsurge of intense anger, despair and acute distress that often erupts during the treatment of a suicidal person may catch the inexperienced therapist by surprise. Professionals tend to be protected from the real life tensions that appear at the height of a suicidal crisis. The therapist's office is too often an ivory tower, protecting the professional from reality.

These intense experiences appear daily in the psychiatric emergency room. Patients come in or are carried in, closer to the peak of their crisis.

It is a different experience to be in the center of the storm, without an emotional buffer from the screams and turmoil.

In 1965, I was assigned to the psychiatric emergency room of the Bronx Municipal Hospital Center, and told to be useful and contribute something. I was welcomed by the members of the medical profession and permitted a wider leeway than is usually afforded psychologists. For that I am still grateful. I began by interviewing and evaluating patients from the log jam of the waiting room, deliberately not omitting those with primarily medical or social problems.

The emergency room functioned under medical auspices and followed a medical model. The availability of an outstanding medical facility, especially in a teaching hospital, was a great advantage but also contained some drawbacks. The least experienced doctors were assigned the most difficult patients.

At that time, all the interviewing in the emergency room was conducted by psychiatric residents, usually in their year of training. The pressure they were under was truly massive. The waiting room was jammed with patients, and as fast as one was taken care of, two more took his or her place. The residents were overworked and faced with responsibilities for which they were often ill prepared. As a result, patients were seen less as individuals in need of help and more as an annoyance. The atmosphere was not conducive to the best assessment and diagnosis. It is a tribute to the trainees and supervisors that the psychiatric and medical work was competent.

My help was warmly appreciated by the residents, who needed all the assistance they could get with their overwhelming case load. In turn, I was provided with all the medical consultation and examinations that were required. These experiences led to an enduring commitment to crisis intervention and the treatment of suicidal people.

THE MANY FACES OF PSYCHIATRIC CRISES

The psychiatric emergency room serves as a suicide and psychopathology prevention center. The emergency room is especially suited for prevention because so many people appear at the height of their crisis, when the proper intervention can have an optimal effect. There is always the possibility then of nipping a pathological process in the bud, of preventing unnecessary breakdowns, suicides, and hospitalizations.

The psychiatric emergency room is a referral and disposition center. For example, elderly suicidal patients who appear in the emergency room as well in the medical clinics and wards of the hospital, are referred to the outpatient psychogeriatric clinic for treatment.

After working in the emergency room, I transferred to the geriatric clinic in 1973. My 17 years of general clinical practice, followed by 7 years in the psychiatric emergency room, helped me appreciate the adaptability and treatment potentials of the suicidal elderly. The crisis and family oriented approaches were particularly valuable, and derived from emergency room practice, even though applied in a different setting.

The psychiatric emergency room serves as an intermediary or go-between for patients in psychotherapy and their therapists. Patients seek and often need the emergency room during a crisis in their ongoing treatment. It was with these patients that I learned about the prevalence of the negative therapeutic reaction (NTR) in therapy. However, it is not generally known how frequently this phenomenon presents in the emergency room and other crisis centers. Bassuk and Birk (1984) estimated that one-third of psychiatric emergency room patients are in concurrent treatment. Unresolved transference and countertransference factors, and major changes in the life situation of the patient or therapist were the most prominent features in precipitating the visits to the emergency room.

In one case, a negative countertransference and then a suicide attempt was precipitated by progress in therapy before the family was ready; in another, by a change in therapist. In this last example, insensitive hospital policies precipitated a suicide.

A poorly handled termination of therapy often precipitated a visit to the emergency room. For example, a patient in the mental hygiene clinic was told by her therapist that her treatment was being terminated. She threatened suicide, and the therapist sent her to the emergency room, where I saw her. I determined she was not suicidal, and did some brief crisis intervention and sent her home. Now, I would have brought the therapist in and perhaps arranged for a family session.

THE EMERGENCY ROOM AS AN INNOVATIVE RESOURCE

The psychiatric emergency room was a center where creative procedures and research activities could be tried out. The very concept of a psychiatric emergency room was a creative innovation.

Some years after I began in the emergency room, a crisis intervention unit was organized, under the direction of a psychiatrist, Dr. Meyer Shimelman, and several psychiatric rehabilitation workers. Basically, they diagnosed the patients, administered medication, saw them briefly, and referred them to the medical hygiene clinic.

The staff conducted an inquiry in which they compared the first 50 patients they saw in crisis intervention with a matched group of 50 patients who were seen routinely by the first year psychiatric residents assigned to the emergency room and referred to the outpatient clinic. The results of this study were dramatic. There was one suicide attempt among those in crisis intervention but no completed suicides. In contrast, there were 8 completed suicides in the 50 who had been referred. It appears that the immediacy of crisis intervention is more valuable than is ordinarily realized.

These suicide figures still sound unbelievable to me. Interestingly enough, however, I came across a similar figure at the inpatient alcohol treatment unit of the hospital. Alcoholics applying there were not accepted if they were also on drugs. Many of them knew that, and concealed their other habits, while those who were honest were turned away. I was informed by a staff member that six of those in the past year who were not accepted killed themselves. Such claims need to be double-checked and the studies replicated, but they stand as an illustration of the desperate situations of those who came for help, and the need for immediate crisis oriented intervention.

Another study (Karasu & Richman, 1972) described the results of minimarathon family crisis intervention in the emergency room. I saw patients in family crisis intervention just once, for a full day from 9 a.m. to 6 p.m. This one meeting led to dramatic results, ranging from an effective preparation for hospitalization or longer term treatment, to the resolution of a suicidal crisis.

Encounter groups and marathon sessions were once a fad, but have lately gone out of style. That is perhaps to be welcomed, since the encounter movement attracted fringe elements who utilized novel approaches more to satisfy their voyeuristic and sadistic urges than for a more enduring healing effect. Nevertheless, some positive lessons were to be gleaned, as we did in the minimarathon crisis intervention study.

The implications of such research extend beyond the confines of the emergency room. A major lesson is that all mental health workers needed to sharpen their diagnostic skills, especially in the areas of danger to the self or others. Another lesson is to institute treatment or hospitalization *immediately* in cases of possible suicide or homicide or other life-threatening conditions.

The crisis intervention concept becomes increasingly valuable in these stressful times when crises almost seem to be the norm rather than the exception. In mental health settings crises are more severe and widespread today than they were in 1965 when I began my crisis intervention work, and there are more patients for whom no facilities are available. According to Dr. Clarence Chen, who, at that time, was Director of the Psychiatric Emergency room at the Bronx Municipal Hospital Center, this is an age of epidemics, the major ones at this writing being AIDS, homelessness, drugs, violence, and a variety of suicidal behaviors.

Those who come for help, especially in such settings as the psychiatric emergency room, represent a high risk population for suicide. The possibilities for urgent yet comprehensive treatment are very promising. One recommendation is for a research department, as part of the psychiatric emergency room and other crisis centers, to keep statistics and conduct systematic studies. A second recommendation is for a crisis intervention team, located in the psychiatric (or general) emergency room.

Not only crisis intervention but family crisis intervention is most often the treatment of choice. The Langsley, Kaplan et al. (1968) group organized a specially trained family crisis team in the emergency room, available on a 24-hour basis. After I had visited their unit in 1967, I believed a family oriented crisis intervention team was needed in all general and psychiatric hospitals. The crisis intervention team could also be available for the inpatient services and the outpatient medical clinics.

Berman and Jacobs (1991) recommend the establishment of a trauma response team that could be available for all school crises in public and high schools, especially crises of suicide. Similar recommendations can be made to set up crisis hot lines for senior centers, adult homes, rehabilitation hospitals, nursing homes, and other facilities for the elderly.

For crisis teams in hospitals and similar locations I would also recommend the establishment of two telephone hot lines. One would be for suicidal people as well as their relatives, friends, and other concerned persons. Another would be available for family physicians and other doctors and health personnel who were faced with a possibly suicidal patient and felt the need for some immediate consultation.

In summary, it is fruitful and life-saving to see suicidal impulses, thoughts, and behavior as communicating the presence of a crisis which is perceived as insoluble by those involved, and to begin family crisis intervention immediately. While successful individual therapy of the suicidal can take place, that can not be accomplished when the family and other significant social network and support persons are determined to sabotage or undermine the therapeutic efforts.

The suicidal elderly are subject to more crises than any other group in the United States. More crisis intervention and outreach services are therefore needed for the suicidal elderly, with more opportunities for continued treatment which will lead to greater opportunities for an enriched existence.

4

Therapy: The
Healing Relationship

Art must make the difficult seem easy.

—Thomas Mann, Letters

THE MULTIDETERMINED APPROACH

Effective psychotherapy of the suicidal elderly rests upon six foundations: a sound knowledge of gerontology; a sound theoretical approach
to suicide; a grasp of the commonalities and basic principles of all psychotherapy of the suicidal; a firm understanding of the healing relationship; a background of training and experience; and the therapist's
ability to deal with the intensity of the experience. This chapter, consequently, deals as much with the therapist as with the patient.

The treatment follows a seven-phase process, from the beginning or
the initial contacts to the end and termination. The steps are summarized in Table 4.1.

In working with the suicidal, the context, especially the family or significant others with their unresolved tensions and conflicts, is a vital
part of the suicidal condition. Suicide can be a response to the wishes or
needs of significant others, as the psychoanalyst Paul Federn pointed
out, on the basis of bitter experience (he eventually killed himself). Reduction of stress in the family and other social systems of which the suicidal person is a part reduces the risk of suicide. The unit of treatment

Table 4.1
The Psychotherapeutic Process

The Initial Phase
Dealing with referrals, first meeting, clarification of ground rules.

Crisis Intervention
Assessment of risk
Assessment and involvement of the suicidal person and the family members. Family crisis intervention.
Pinpointing the crisis; evaluation of suicidal risk; determination of disposition (e.g., hospitalization or outpatient);
Determination of target symptoms and a tentative treatment plan.
Intervention. Crisis intervention may be sufficient, or else the contact continues into the next stage.

Early Phase of Continuing Therapy
Continuation of crisis intervention and assessment, including "monitoring" and further clarification of target goals and target symptoms.
Establishing rapport and commitment.

The First Crisis in Therapy
Re-arousal of separation anxiety.
The negative therapeutic reaction.

Repeated Crises in Therapy
Continued monitoring of symptoms or danger signs.
Dealing with discouragement, scapegoating, and sabotage.

Dealing with Special and Typical Problems
Contacts with outside agencies, hospitals, caregivers, therapists and other professionals.
Constructive use of transference and (especially) countertransference.
Resolution.

The Ending Phase
Importance of timing and possible arousal of separation anxiety.
Termination.
Arrangement for periodic follow-up.

must be broadened, therefore, well beyond the confines of the traditional medical model.

Because of the ubiquity of unbearable separation and loss experiences in the family that were not dealt with at the time they occurred, the suicidal person is expressing the tension and unfinished tasks of an entire family system. The first goal of therapy, therefore, is the reduction of tension and separation anxiety in the entire family.

The problem is that the medical point of view singles out one individual as the only patient, with sometimes the unfortunate result that the therapist may omit others who are intimately involved. As used in this book therefore, "patient" may refer to an individual, to a family, or to some other unit of which the patient is a part. The unit depends upon the nature of the therapeutic task.

The value of psychotherapy for the depressed elderly has only recently become recognized. The National Institute of Mental Health (NIMH) "Consensus Development Conference on the Diagnosis and Treatment of Depression in Late Life" (Ferguson, 1991) demonstrated that cognitive, behavioral, interpersonal, and psychodynamic psychotherapies were successful in the treatment of major depression in the elderly. Even before this landmark conference, psychotherapy was and has remained a major treatment method with depressed and suicidal persons, although biological interventions were on the increase.

Missing from the conference were studies on crisis intervention, group therapy, family therapy, and suicide. In practice, these different approaches are often combined with the individual therapy that was presented. Consequently, there is good reason for everyone involved with the suicidal elderly to become familiar with all the psychotherapeutic methods which are used most frequently and considered most effective.

It is unfortunate that the suicidal patient is neglected in the growing body of writings on the psychotherapy of depression and other disturbances in late life. The literature describes procedures which are applicable to the treatment of the suicidal elderly. I surveyed the literature on psychotherapy and suicide in general, including the research on cognitive behavior therapy (Beck and his colleagues, 1979) and interpersonal therapy (Klerman and his colleagues, 1984). Also included were Boss, (1963), Maltsberger, (1986, 1991) and other analytic writers, the systemic, family, and group therapists, and paradoxical therapists.

I singled out studies of major depression in late life because its treatment has been most thoroughly researched and because that group may be closest to elderly suicidal subjects. The majority of the suicidal elderly who committed suicide are diagnosed as depressed (Murphy & Wetzel, 1990). I interpolated from descriptions of younger patients to the elderly and from psychotherapy with the elderly in general to the suicidal elderly in particular.

The literature was supplemented by interviews with colleagues and my own notes and recollections. These were the most valuable for identifying the commonalities of actual clinical practice. By commonalities I mean events, features, or dynamics that are present in the treatment of the majority of suicidal elderly patients. A second purpose of the literature review was to see what areas need to be more thoroughly explored.

The differences in therapies are not to be denied. Successful therapists, unlike happy families, are not all alike. Some are directive, others nondirective; some are technique oriented, others relationship oriented. These are different but not necessarily mutually exclusive approaches, since the same therapist may respond differently at different times, depending upon the circumstances, and sometimes their results are different.

Differences in outcome are also found. The NIMH sponsored studies, for example, reported that depressed patients with personality disorders did better with cognitive behavior therapy, depressed patients without a personality disorder did better with interpersonal therapy (Shea, Pilkonis, Beckham, Collins, et al., 1990), and those with vegetative symptoms did better with medication. The correct fit between patient, treatment, and therapist is important. In spite of these differences, all approaches report success, in terms of an improvement in functioning and symptom relief. The research studies support these claims.

Jerome Frank (1973) suggested that there are nonspecific factors that help account for the success of psychotherapy, such as the nature of the relationship and the presence of empathy. By "nonspecific," he seems to have meant features that are not technique-dependent. These are not to be discounted or explained away as "nonspecific," but rather to be welcomed as evidence that human resources or relationships may be at least as important as the application of techniques.

A second explanation is experience. Fiedler (1950) found that experienced therapists from different schools were more similar to each other whatever their theoretical orientation, while inexperienced therapists were dissimilar, in accordance with the theoretical positions of their schools. In other words, there are more commonalities found among experienced therapists.

These studies do not apply directly to elderly suicidal people. We have no way of knowing how elderly suicidal people might have fared because the treatment of the elderly suicidal person is omitted in published research or clinical reports, except as an incidental reference or case history.

Valuable information about elderly suicide is found in the many publications on demography and epidemiology of elderly suicide (McIntosh, 1992). The major risk factors have been identified. The problem is that the mental and physical illnesses, social isolation, crucial life events, and other conditions generally associated with suicide in the elderly also occur with great frequency in the non-suicidal elderly.

However, the treatment conclusions reached from demographic and epidemiological studies are often discouraging, invalid, and even absurd. The usual recommendations for younger suicidal persons include a dynamic and psychotherapeutic approach in their treatment which, of course, is sensible and valid. In contrast, the recommendations for the elderly suicidal are for medication, electric shock therapy, referral to senior centers, and institutionalization. For example, Stewart (1991), on the treatment of depression in the elderly including those who are suicidal, declared that treatment options include different drug therapies and ECT. There was not a mention of psychotherapy.

Medication and other physical therapies and institutionalization are at least forms of treatment. There is another movement, which I find has ominous undertones, to encourage death for the terminally ill, assisted by physicians if necessary. The terminally ill who are suicidal are labeled as quite different from other living human organisms, with their death being an act of compassion.

I do not advocate forcing people to live past their time, but other measures than assisted suicide are preferable. An example is the positive effects of marital therapy with the terminally ill (Richman, 1981), not only for the dying person but the family, and I will have more to say about the topic later. At this time, assisted suicide for the terminally ill is too much intertwined with generally negative and biased attitudes towards the elderly who need help.

Either directly or implicitly, the suicidal elderly are presented as unsuitable for psychotherapy. These unfounded conclusions are reached even though the suicidal elderly have been neglected, not only as psychotherapy patients, but as the subjects of research studies of psychotherapy. Such conclusions are very questionable.

Fortunately, the literature combined with clinical experience highlight nine commonalities in psychotherapy which apply to the treatment of the suicidal elderly. These are summarized briefly in the following review followed by a discussion of their clinical applications.

A REVIEW OF TREATMENT COMMONALITIES

1. *A universal agreement is on the importance of a positive doctor–patient relationship.* The value of the relationship is emphasized, even when there

are significant differences in the treatment procedures and the activity levels of the therapists.

2. *A related commonality is the presence of a caring and hopeful attitude in the therapist.* Silove, Parker, and Manicavasagar (1990) found that "perceived therapist care" was strongly associated with satisfaction with therapy by the patient. This "perceived care" is a genuine caring in the therapist, for suicidal persons are exquisitely and accurately attuned to indifference or rejection.

3. *Third was the availability of the therapist in time of need.* Flexibility, availability, and the danger of burnout are the major reasons for the therapist to avoid a case overload. Unfortunately, as we shall see, the rules of many institutions disregard the importance of availability and continuity, sometimes with lethal consequences for the patient.

4. *Fourth was the ability to deal with setbacks and the negative therapeutic reaction (NTR).* The NTR is a predictable phenomenon in the therapy of suicidal persons, no matter what the treatment modality or the age of the client. I attribute that to the perceived threat of successful therapy to the family system, but whatever the reason, the phenomenon is ubiquitous. Without naming it as such, several writers reported the same phenomenon.

5. *Be prepared to deal with problems around separation, loss, and termination.* These areas have been emphasized and described by every investigator who has engaged personally in the treatment of the suicidal and their successful resolution is central to treatment.

The need of both the patient and the other family members to preserve the current homeostasis, no matter how terrible the status quo may seem, is not primarily based upon preventing change but in preventing separation. The fear of change is a reaction to the threat of separation. The *threat* must be emphasized. Anxiety over separation is the key to suicide and reduction of separation anxiety the key to its treatment. And with suicide, separation anxiety is closely connected to death anxiety.

6. *The death trend was a common theme, first described by Moss and Hamilton (1957) as an accumulation of losses and deaths at the time of the suicidal state.* Since the publication of their paper, the "death trend" has become a familiar and often recognized phenomenon. Jacobs (1971) added that it occurs on top of a lifelong history of loss, reaching a crescendo at a

crucial or vulnerable time. This last loss is seen as the last straw, leading to the suicidal act. In my experience, the death trend is also a trend in the family, often handed down from one generation to the next in an often inexplicable, dramatic, and almost mystical manner.

7. *A related problem area is the ubiquity of grief, and the need of the therapist to be alert to and deal with problems around mourning.* The inability to grieve and failures in the grief process are found in the majority of suicidal persons.

8. *The availability of social support systems outside the therapeutic relationship was a commonality in all types of successful therapy.* When these are not present, therapy with the suicidal is more difficult, but still possible. Group psychotherapy is particularly valuable in providing experiences of social belonging and cohesion and a restoration of self esteem.

A review of the commonalities in treatment combined with the resources available to the therapist as well as the patient lead to the last commonality.

9. *Most therapists experienced in the effective psychotherapy of the suicidal elderly prepare a treatment plan.* I cannot imagine treating the suicidal without a competent, comprehensive, and thorough evaluation, and an intervention that is correspondingly broad.

Diane Wood Middlebrook (1991), wrote a biography of Anne Sexton, the eminent poet, which was based in large part upon transcripts of 300 hours of therapy sessions. These were obtained from her psychiatrist, Dr. Martin Orne, with the permission and approval of Ms. Sexton's daughter, Linda Gray Sexton, who was her literary executor. While the use of this material aroused a storm of controversy, the positive and important contribution stood out, as did its sensitive understanding of the suicidal forces and the life forces in Anne Sexton. I consider this book a major contribution to humanistic understanding. Ms. Middlebrook convincingly presented the comprehensive approach to understanding and assessment, broadly defined, with the help of several eminent psychiatrists. "An overview of her case," she wrote, "would distinguish at least three different possible sources: biological, psychological, and sociological" (p. 37). Many of her symptoms, plus evidence of breakdowns on both sides of her family, supported a genetic and biologically based illness.

The psychological factors were legion. The primary one as I saw it, was her need for mothering. For example, Ms. Sexton told Dr. Orne, "I knew I was dependent—but Mother didn't want to be motherly. I clung to her" (Middlebrook, 1991, p. 37). There was much evidence that both her heavily-drinking mother and alcoholic father were dominated by their own unresolved needs for mothering, which they could not acknowledge, possibly even to themselves.

A comprehensive approach is particularly needed in these days, when the biological components of emotional distress and mental illness are emphasized with a corresponding reliance upon medication and physical methods of treatment of suicidal states and related conditions. There has often been a neglect of the psychological and social contributions to suicide. A treatment plan helps the therapist become more aware of significant areas that he or she may have overlooked. Any one-sided emphasis or neglect of possible determinants is to be criticized, whether of the biological or the psychological or some other approach to the exclusion of others.

Lesnoff-Caravaglia (1987) is one of the few gerontologists who responded appropriately to any one-determinant or intervention arguments to explain suicide in the elderly. For example, to the all-too-frequent statement, in both the professional journals and the popular media, that terminal illness is a necessary and sufficient cause of suicide in the elderly, the author states:

> There is generally more than one precipitating reason for suicide in old age. For example, no person kills himself because of a terminal illness. He kills himself because of the pain it would cause him (which can be handled in some instances), the emotional drain his family would bear (family counseling might alleviate this), the financial problems that might result (proper financial backing could be made available), the desire to be remembered as he was in health (psychiatric care might address this), the wish to control when death will occur (physicians could counsel). All can have points of intervention. This is the form suicide prevention must take for older persons (p. 278).

In effect, the response to suicidal thoughts in the elderly is the availability of competent health professionals with extensive training and skills in the different therapeutic approaches. The experienced therapist resorts to a variety of procedures depending upon the situation, rather than relying exclusively upon any one approach. Often, he or she is part of a team where different skills and knowledge are available and shared.

Hendin (1991) recommends a knowledge of the psychodynamics of suicide as an aid in assessment, for example, in an evaluation of the nature and intensity of the prevailing emotions, and exploration of the meanings of death, and the deeper, often unconscious roots of the suicidal state. A knowledge of psychodynamics is valuable for all therapists who treat the suicidal, whether or not their treatment orientation is dynamically oriented. The dynamics help the therapist in understanding and in conveying an empathic understanding of the suicidal urge to the patient. It advances the therapeutic alliance and helps the therapist to avoid intervening in a non-therapeutic manner.

THE HEALING RELATIONSHIP

The relationship commonalities in practice appear as the presence of rapport and commitment, transference (TR) and countertransference (CTR), and their vicissitudes. Rapport basically refers to positive regard between people. Commitment is based upon the therapists' caring and willingness to accept the professional responsibilities of the task, learn the skills, and accept the anxieties and tensions that may accompany such work. Despair and giving up on the patient are the enemies of commitment, while a hopeful attitude is its ally. What is said here about individuals applies as well to families, to other groups, and even to society.

A healing relationship potentiates the dormant growth and caring forces that are awakened in the meeting of the patient with the therapist. Such relationships permit the release of health-promoting and life-enhancing forces. That does not mean love is enough; love is not enough, but it is basic. Professional treatment is also not enough, but it is basic.

The suicidal urge is overcome through a fruitful partnership of therapeutic skills, the assets of the suicidal person, the relationship between both, and a caring environment outside the treatment setting. For this purpose the family, social network, or other groups may be a pivotal part of the treatment. I have found that it is not possible to be neutral when confronted with a suicidal old person. Neutrality, in the face of a wish to die, is undesirable. Like a blank expression, it is perceived as indifference, disapproval, or self-preoccupation.

When someone expresses a desire to end it all, I place myself actively on the side of life. I explore options or alternatives, the tensions involved behind the suicidal state, and the measures necessary to reduce them. I ask people to call should they be in acute crisis, and I remain available. An essential ingredient in the healing relationship with the therapist is a working alliance with the family, even when they are not present.

The doctor–patient roles are to be respected, but the healing relationship implies a human and humane approach. One can sometimes have a cup of coffee with the patients, bring them chocolates, or provide sheer human companionship. Such a relationship is consistent with a professional attitude in the therapist. Being a patient in a positive sense is a role that sometimes has to be learned. Being a patient can sometimes be a life pattern in a negative sense. It maintains the person in a dysfunctional role, while the roles of other family members become correspondingly undesirable and subtly limiting. This might be considered seeing the person as a patient when it is not appropriate. Fortunately, the professional and the appropriate patient roles are compatible with growth and with being human.

To be human means that the therapist is present with the person, group, or family, and the patient is also present. To be present means to be involved and committed. To be professional means acquiring a background of learning and experience, and an application of the principles of one's craft. To be both human and professional means becoming the best therapist that one can be.

The relationship between mutual respect and of being both human and professional extends beyond the confines of the consultation room. Roberts (1985), for example, criticized the lack of respect sometimes displayed by psychologists towards those with whom they disagree. He suggested that how well psychologists treated each other was a measure of how caring and professional they were.

Therapy for the suicidal is problem and solution oriented. Suicide is based upon a problem in the present which seems insoluble to those involved. All one needs to do is identify and resolve the problem, and there is no more suicide. The crisis intervention orientation, with which all treatment of the suicidal begins, is maintained throughout treatment. The deceptively simple recommendation for problem resolution is accomplished through a competent assessment, the healing relationship, the respect for the abilities of the patient, the use of other therapeutic procedures as needed, such as medication, the involvement of social agencies, and working with the family and, of course, following appropriate treatment procedures as described in this and other chapters.

In therapy, as in art, to make the difficult seem easy requires a lot of work. Effective therapy requires a knowledge of how and when to intervene and how and when *not* to intervene. In *Restoration*, a novel by Rose Tremain, there is a scene in which a doctor—actually a medical student—is asked to cure the king's spaniel, which is dying, but the student gets drunk and passes out. However, the dog is dying because of all the treatment he has been receiving and recovers because he was left alone and given a chance to recuperate.

The point for therapy is to avoid intervening when that would interfere with the treatment or the family interaction process. Noninterference, however, is the opposite of being passive or unresponsive. The therapist does not fall asleep, as did Tremain's medical student, but instead is actively listening and actively present.

I agree with Sandler (1982) who emphasizes the focus upon current relationships and problems in the psychotherapy of the elderly, but it is not important whether to emphasize the past or the present; that depends upon the nature of the case. Most of the time I leave that to the patient. I do so, because of my faith in the accumulated knowledge, wisdom, and experience of older suicidal patients and their ability to grow in therapy.

The focus of the relationship is on understanding and acceptance, which in turn is based upon a respect for both the individual and the family system. This includes all the family members, without trying to impose change or extrinsic values, but working in partnership with them. These are essential ingredients in the treatment of the suicidal elderly.

Such acceptance is consistent with the latest developments in therapy. Reichelt and Christiansen (1990) note a change in attitude, from questioning as a basis for interpretation by the therapist, to questioning in order to promote self-understanding in the client.

This attitude is consistent with the belief of de Shazar and his colleagues (1988) that all people have the potential for solving their problems, and that the solution emerges from the patient. While their "solution oriented school" cannot be considered non-directive, their therapy "can be seen as built on the assumption that the client constructs his or her own solution based on his or her own resources and successes" (1988, p. 50). That sounds close to a client-centered approach.

The change in attitude also corresponds with the view that there are inherent forces of growth, love, and caring in the family as well as in the individual. These attitudes are closer to that of client-centered therapy (Rogers, 1951) than most people have recognized. As Fowers (1990) said, "The beauty of a systemic approach to marital therapy is that it allows the therapist to respect both partners' viewpoints through seeing each spouse's actions as complimentary aspects of a pattern that is mutually determined" (p. 27).

All psychotherapy can be considered 'a pattern that is mutually determined' through the influences of the transference and countertransference. Commitment and rapport are essential ingredients of the working alliance, and these, in turn, are aspects of transference and countertransference.

THE LIFE REVIEW AND THE SUICIDAL ELDERLY

Butler (1963) has pointed out the value of reminiscing in the positive adaptations of the elderly. It can serve as a means of looking over the entirety of a life and tying it all together. Reminiscing then becomes a major means for achieving the ego integrity which Erikson (1950) described as the crowning developmental phase. Erikson and the life review are spiritual companions. The reminiscence process has been formalized and given a structure, which has been called "Life-Review Therapy."

The life review is valuable at all ages, not only with the elderly. Dan Levinson and his colleagues (1978), have reported its appearance during the life crises of middle-aged men. I have seen it occur in children too, as young as age 5, with a therapeutic effect.

The five-year-old, the youngest in her family, was able to integrate her dim memories of a grandmother who died when the girl was two, and as a result to feel more a part of the family. All the other family members had spoken at length about grandma and what she had meant to them. It is important, and a vital reason for the elderly to refrain from committing suicide, that they become part of the life review of others which, in a sense, becomes part of their immortality.

The life review has not been recommended for those whose lives have been so traumatic that such a procedure might become unbearably painful. One 60-year-old woman, for example, attributed her "nervous breakdown" to seeing a therapist "who forced me to remember everything."

Nevertheless, I have found that the life review can be valuable to every suicidal person in therapy, when properly and judiciously applied. The memory and review of traumatic events can become the basis for mourning deaths and other events in the past, which in turn can free the person from those traumatic shackles and enable a more enriched life to emerge. In the process a person's defenses, such as denial, must be respected. Life-review therapy requires an awareness of when not to intervene or force someone to remember everything, and when to be a good and facilitating listener. In other words, life-review therapy follows the principles and procedures of all good psychotherapy.

COUNTERTRANSFERENCE WITH THE SUICIDAL ELDERLY

To maintain the therapeutic relationship, the therapist must understand and be in touch with his or her countertransference. Such understanding, however, is often very difficult and even painful. It may require supervision, consultation, the presence of solid support systems, and perhaps personal therapy.

It is a major commonality in the therapeutic process with suicidal people for a negative transference to take place. The misunderstanding of that event can occasion many difficulties, including a reactive negative countertransference. What is said about the transference of the patient applies as well to the countertransference of the therapist. They can be a mirror image of each other. There can be a negative countertransference reaction in the therapist, with covert demands that the patient or family follow the therapist's directives or value system. That is countertransference, unrecognized as it may be.

> Buchanan and Lappin (1990) described the angry and rejecting reaction of a family therapist, Eileen, in her mid 20's, towards Louise, a 63-year-old black grandmother who was taking care of the child of her drug-addicted daughter. The grandmother had had it. She condemned both her disrespectful and problematic grandson and the covertly blaming attitude of the therapist for the grandmother's scapegoating of the child.
>
> The family therapy team had been observing the session behind a one-way screen. They buzzed the therapist to take a break and consult with them. With amazing speed Eileen changed her attitude in a more compassionate and understanding direction and returned to the family session. Quickly, she established a therapeutic alliance and began the process of healing.

It took me 10 years of intensive work with suicidal patients and families combined with personal psychotherapy and a constant self-examination of my countertransference to reach the level that Eileen obtained in 10 minutes. The speed with which skill was established may have been exaggerated in their report. However, the message that supervision and consultation must be immediately available for those treating suicidal and related conditions is well taken. The availability of such help has saved lives and prevented much grief.

Transference and countertransference arise from different, even though universal, experiences and their meanings and functions are different even though intimately related. Just as the fate of the transference plays a discernible role in the outcome of treatment, so does the countertransference of the therapist and how it is handled.

The Meanings of Countertransference

Transference and countertransference have fluid meanings and definitions, but they all refer to a relationship. In 1910 Freud defined countertransference as the patient's influence on the unconscious feelings of the analyst (Freud, 1957). In 1912 Freud (1958) added that the patient's unconscious communicates with the unconscious of the therapist, who is thereby enabled to reconstruct the patient's unconscious.

The concept of countertransference has since been broadened by some psychoanalysts to include the *totality* of feelings and other reactions towards the patient aroused in the therapist on both a conscious and unconscious level (Heiman, 1950). Heiman's more comprehensive concept has been increasingly accepted in psychoanalysis, for example by Abend (1989), Feiner and Epstein (1979), Slakter (1987), and Strean (1991).

The concept of countertransference can be broadened still further to include groups and societies. Freud's discovery of the Oedipus complex implied a family system of relationships and fantasies which was largely outside of consciousness. However, he did not follow his theory to the logical conclusion of a family unconscious, although he did consider unconscious group processes in his paper on group psychology (Freud, 1955).

Applied to families, countertransference includes the feelings and reactions of the therapist to the personalities and provocations of family members and other significant persons, *whether or not they are present.* That includes the mutual influences of the unconscious of the therapist with the unconscious of the family members.

The contributions of investigators outside the psychoanalytic framework have contributed to the development of the concepts of transference and countertransference which is presented here. On the basis of their systemic studies of communication, Watzlawick, Beavin, and Jackson (1967) emphasized that communications are not linear, from a sender to a receiver. Instead, they are reciprocal and circular.

Applying this view to psychotherapy, the transactions between the unconscious of the therapist with the unconscious of the patient and their reciprocal nature help explain the extraordinary insights displayed by some gifted therapists and the astonished remarks of some patients, of "How did you know that?" Similar intuitions and insights are expressed by patients, many of whom seem to read my mind and to say what I had been thinking.

Bias as Countertransference

The broader definition of countertransference is not only part of the direct relationship or interaction between the patient and therapist. It refers to such phenomena as ageism, those biased attitudes towards the elderly, as determined by personal anxieties and conflicts on the one hand, and social stereotypes, myths, and prejudices on the other. Many people consider psychoanalysis to be a victim as well as a perpetrator of such ageism.

Freud may actually have inhibited subsequent analytic investigations because of his belief that the older person was not amenable to psychoanalysis. He thought that the requisite mental elasticity was lacking over the age of 50. "Old people are no longer educable" (1953, p. 264) was what he said. That was part of his countertransference, based upon ageism. Freud's ageism also applied to himself. He was convinced that he would not live past the age of 50, which was probably both a wish and a fear. At least he was consistent in his ageism.

Because of Freud's influence, a generally negative view of aging has prevailed among many analysts. One analyst, for example, described the elderly as characterized by "a fixed and rigid habit of adjustment. . . . Problems of adaptation that have not been previously mastered successfully become too much of a burden for failing psychological and physical powers. . . . The elders are being left behind by life. They as individuals can experience this only as a desertion. . . . There is increasing sensitiveness to slights, increasing querulousness" (Gitelson, 1975, pp. 578–580). The author was referring to the elderly in general, and not to psychopathology. Such statements are remarkably one-sided and omit vital facts about the rich lives and personalities of many aged people.

I do not know how much of Gitelson's views were derived from actual experience in psychotherapy with the elderly, but they do not correspond to mine or the experiences of several other practitioners, including Payne (1975). However, as Kastenbaum and Ross (1975) noted, psychoanalysis is not to be singled out for criticism. Psychoanalysis is but one example of a more general neglect of the elderly by the entire mental health field. Studies of social attitudes are consistent with the belief that the avoidance is related to the association of aging with physical and mental decline, loss—especially the loss of sexual pow-ers—and the unconscious continuation of early parent-child conflicts.

These are all reflected in the countertransference of many therapists. Clarke (1981) studied countertransference reactions towards the dying. Cooper (1984) also considered issues of loss and death in group psycho-therapy with the aged. It is evident that those therapists who find it most difficult to deal with the ill or frail elderly are those who have not come to terms with their own fears of death and illness.

Despite Freud and social prejudices, psychoanalysts were treating older patients almost from the first (Abraham, 1953). More recently, Mahler (1968), Erikson (1950), Klein (1975) and others have demon-strated that psychoanalytic theory, too, can develop and progress and that this progress can apply to the elderly. Erikson expanded the con-cept of development to encompass the entire life span, with each stage having its age-appropriate crises and tasks. In adolescence, for example, the task and the danger is the development of ego autonomy versus identity diffusion. The tasks of the last two stages of life are generativity versus stagnation, followed by ego integrity versus despair and disgust.

Countertransference and Society

There are forces in the world which can also be seen as exemplifying ageist prejudices. For example, there is a series of social beliefs which see old age purely as a time of decline, illness, sexual impotence, physi-cal weakness, mental senility, and approaching death. These can be seen as the societal analogues of disgust and despair.

The proponents of such views ignore the assets of the elderly, the in-crements in knowledge, experience, wisdom, and, as some of us have discovered, humor. The success of how-to-commit-suicide books such as *Final Exit*, and the California State referendum to legally permit phy-sicians to kill terminally ill patients at the patient's request, can lead to a subtle avoidance or mishandling of the older depressed and suicidal pa-tient. Such books and measures represent society's negative CTR which threatens to undermine the positive CTR which has led to social secu-rity, medicare, senior centers, and the lowering of the elderly suicidal rate, prior to 1980.

Countertransference and the Sexually Active Elderly

Gurian (1986) explored another major countertransference area which he called "the myth of the aged as asexual." Negative attitudes towards the elderly appear because older people are perceived as close to death and, paradoxically, because the elderly insist upon being alive and sexual.

It is indeed difficult to see a sexually active person primarily in terms of decline and approaching death. The actively engaged elderly person throws unexamined prejudices into question, disturbing the stereotype, thereby confronting biased people who are cognitively rigid with a form of cognitive dissonance they cannot tolerate.

> Stanley M., age 75, had a very distant relationship in response to a warm and emotionally demanding wife. One night, however, he had a very passionate sexual experience with her, which followed some discussion with his therapist. He returned for his next therapy session in a state of great distress. He complained that he had been like a young boy and that this was unseemly for an elderly man. A few months later he reported with great relief that these sexual urges no longer "bothered" him.

This positive sexual experience was a potential turning point in Mr. M.'s development which he, sadly, was not ready for. In some elderly people, however, this conflict can have a positive result.

> Laura E., a 73-year-old chronically depressed widow, was exploring the ramifications of a widow's life. She recalled a friend whose husband died. Two months later this friend was at a senior center, dancing. Someone admonished her for dancing so soon after her husband's death. "He's dead, I'm not," she replied. My widowed patient thought her friend had a point.

Sex can be enjoyed at all ages, whether in thought or action. The point is conveyed in the story of a physician who is examining a patient. "Are you ever bothered by sexual thoughts or fantasies?" asked the doctor. "No, I rather enjoy them," said the patient.

An avoidance of sexual issues in the elderly is especially frequent in the younger therapist. This countertransference problem can be active, even when sex is ostensibly dealt with.

> Nancy P., age 67, complained bitterly of her husband's excessive sexual demands and how painful sex was for her. Since she had just been diagnosed as having cancer of the rectum and was being treated with chemotherapy, it seemed sensible to side with her, and suggest to her 75-year-old husband that he reduce his demands. Paradoxically, the intervention enabled the therapist to avoid dealing with the couple's problems around intimacy.

The avoidance of sexual issues by the therapist can generalize to the avoidance of dealing with other expressions of affection such as touching and making physical contact, and with all positive feelings or experiences.

STRESS IN THE THERAPIST

The commonalities found in the treatment of the suicidal help explain the difficulties encountered and the intensity of the TR and CTR reactions. The seriously suicidal person is attempting to deal with the basic themes of life and death, with loss, separation, and other life crises made still more unbearable because of the inability to mourn past losses. Because of past experiences, and unexplored beliefs and assumptions, the suicidal patient and family often distrust the entire treatment process, including the hospital and the therapist, and they often expect that they will be disappointed and abandoned. They undermine therapy, even to the point of completing suicide, as though to prove that their attitudes were valid.

During therapy, therefore, the nature of stress appears in all its horrible glory, *especially when it is being successful.* If the therapist can deal with these events, therapy is both successful for the suicidal patient and rewarding for the therapist.

A positive attitude toward the patient and family by the therapist occurs through a combination of intrinsic qualities in the self of the therapist and the effects of training and experience. The therapist's commitment, warmth, and acceptance are one part of this positive regard. As another part, the therapist does not blame or criticize the patient or family. These positive features are all potentially life saving.

At best, however, the encounter with severely suicidal people and their families can be extremely trying. Most distressing is the turmoil of feelings aroused in the therapist in response to the intensity of the rage, anxiety, and depression expressed verbally and non-verbally. These reactions usually occur in an atmosphere of unrelieved tension and the imminent eruption of primitive drives and affects, and overall in the shadow of threatened violence and death. Bongar (1991) has discussed in detail both the emotional effects and legal effects of a suicide on the therapist. The anxiety arousal by the possibility of such a death is part of the situation.

What is not always recognized is that extreme eruptions signal a crisis in the family system. Their appearance in therapy is different from such explosive interactions at home. There are therapeutic potentials in the treatment setting, which the perceptive therapist will seize upon. The eruption of primitive rage and violence occurs most frequently during the opening session. That intense encounter is usually a positive sign.

> Rachel W., a 78-year-old widow, had continued to work actively and was noted for her energy, intelligence, and ability. She was an unusually domineering woman who maintained a tight control over her divorced daughter and four grandchildren, and was locked into an intense conflict with her daughter over who was the better mother of the grandchildren.
>
> However Mrs. W. began to experience lapses in memory and increased difficulties at work. She and her family ignored these problems and continued their lifelong pattern of intergenerational competition and conflict. But one Mother's Day Mrs. W. refused to go out to dinner with the rest of the family, expecting a long period of urging and arguments. Instead they left without her. Mrs. W. attempted suicide.
>
> After discharge from the hospital, she was seen in a family session with her daughter and grandchildren. The session consisted largely of intense shouting matches between the patient and her daughter, with the grandchildren siding seemingly with the grandmother, but at the same time, being manifestly frightened.
>
> The therapist commended them for expressing themselves so well and for being so open and honest. He complimented them further for fulfilling their roles as patients. He then brought up the possible difficulties Mrs. W. might be experiencing. Although not stated directly, the family seemed astonished that they all left together in a friendly manner, despite the intense blowup.
>
> Mrs. W. phoned a few days later to say that her daughter had called and that they had had a friendly chat. She also accepted her daughter's friendly invitation to visit them. She is continuing to work. However, she refused to continue therapy on the grounds that there was no need.

For an intense argument to take place without destructive consequences can be therapeutic. The greater the intensity of the anger, scapegoating, double binding, and other destructive interactions during a family therapy session with a suicidal patient, the greater the opportunity for clearing the air, and reducing stress and the anxiety over separation and loss. I feel more uncomfortable when a session with a suicidal person is quiet and free of conflict, especially early in the treatment and when the family is present.

Bereavement, or more accurately, unresolved mourning, is ubiquitous in the treatment of the suicidal elderly. The death of a loved one escalates the danger of suicide in someone who is vulnerable. Early recognition and referral to the properly trained and committed therapist can make all the difference.

However, dealing with death, and therefore grief, is one of the major tasks of the elderly that is avoided by most therapists. The therapist's own losses and unfinished mourning, as well as her or his own vulnerability and awareness of mortality, are major aspects of the countertransference. Yet such personal experiences may foster a greater understanding and make one a better therapist.

The well-qualified therapist has confronted and overcome problems around loss, bereavement, aging, illness, and other life and death issues. Ageism can enter in despite the best intentions on the part of the therapist to be free of such prejudices. That is why continuing consultation and supervision are recommended.

The Difficult Patient

Dealing with the refractory suicidal patient is an area of concern, no matter what the treatment method. Difficult patients are those who do not respond to therapy or the therapist, and who often continue on an inexorable downward course, sometimes to suicide. Akiskal (1991) discusses difficult patients in the context of a largely biological approach. For example, he defines "a resistant depressive" as someone who does not respond despite treatment with two kinds of antidepressants. In the context of a psycho-educational approach he defines "intractable" patients as those who are difficult to manage clinically. Whatever the approach, such patients are seen by the committed therapist.

What can be done, aside from labeling them as difficult or untreatable? The primary recommendation is to, above all, not give up. That means an ability to listen to older persons without taking the resistance personally, to recognize and appreciate their contributions to understanding and solutions to life problems on the basis of the accumulated experience of age, and to accept their decisions, whatever they may be. The majority of suicidal people respond positively to such psychotherapy. However, that may be easier to say than to practice.

The confrontation with a difficult patient who is also a high suicide risk arouses fear and other unpleasant feelings in the therapist. These are appropriate to the circumstances. In fact, the beginning therapist who does not react with such strong feelings is probably not a good therapist; and the therapist, beginner or not, who avoids such feelings, is especially not a good therapist for the suicidal. As Zuk (1990) said in reference to the conflict cycle seen predictably in all family therapy, "Of course, one had to be able to take the heat and believe that the heat was critical to understanding what was going on and how one might be helpful" (p. 38).

With the elderly, a professional relationship entails respect for what the patient has to offer and the ability to make use of the patient's assets. After many years of working with the elderly, the value of their knowledge, wisdom, and experience has been brought home over and over again. Nevertheless, it is still advisable to maintain an optimal distance, and a professional rather than a social relationship.

The Negative Therapeutic Reaction

The negative therapeutic reaction (NTR) is one of the most important commonalities in all treatment with the suicidal, both inpatient and outpatient. It is best understood as a crisis, specifically a crisis in therapy. Progress proceeds through a series of such crises, setbacks, and NTRs followed by further growth and maturity.

Earlier I presented the healing effect of a therapist's availability combined with empathy and acceptance in the treatment of a severely psychotic and suicidal patient as described by Boss (1963). The therapist also described how this patient improved, then regressed, then improved "dozens of times," and finally recovered. This was the NTR in action. Boss attributed the setbacks and the process of recovery to his patient's struggle with accepting her mature, sensual womanhood.

Other therapists, not as perceptive as Boss, have interpreted the NTR as signalling a failure in treatment. I suspect that many of the suicides reported by Bloom (1967), which he attributed to the hostility and death wishes of the therapist, were based upon the crisis in treatment which was precipitated by a NTR because of the threat of success.

The NTR assumes a variety of different forms, usually not recognized as an anxiety reaction in the family to the threat of improvement.

Elizabeth Swados (1991) described her own negative, angry, and rejecting reaction when her chronically depressed and suicidal mother, when hospitalized, became less symptomatic and more relaxed, but also willing to give up the mature woman role which she artificially assumed before the outside world. Ms. Swados did not seem to recognize the threat to her own customary roles and relationships.

Somatization in the relatives as well as anger are other NTR reactions. An example could be seen in the family of Anne Sexton. She was profoundly depressed and suicidal, but responded dramatically in psychotherapy. As she improved, her mother responded with a "withering" rejection and refused to pay for her college education. Mother, then developed a malignant breast cancer and underwent a radical mastectomy.

In both the Swados and Sexton families there were also forces of love, caring, and growth, as there are in most of the families where suicidal behavior occurs. The following chapter, on family therapy, discusses these positive family resources in depth and how they can be used in therapy with patients like Mrs. Swados and Anne Sexton.

It is because of the family dynamics that the NTR in response to positive experiences in therapy becomes a major hazard. Nevertheless, the NTR is being discussed here as a component of all therapy with the suicidal, not only family therapy. That is because the family members are in the office, whether or not they are physically present, and every member of the family is responding to the fears of separation and the dissolution of the family system. The anxieties that are acted out in the therapy of suicidal people are family anxieties.

The therapeutic crisis, which goes by the name of the NTR, is based upon the interaction between events in treatment and their repercussions throughout the family system. Relapses are much more serious in the case of suicidal people, and therefore that much more to be anticipated and prepared for.

Sometimes, the NTR may cover up the importance of the doctor–patient relationship, partly because such relationships are believed to represent a form of disloyalty to the family. An example in my earlier work involved a 19-year-old who was seemingly rejecting and unrelated to his therapist. His extreme and suicidal reaction when the therapist left was a surprise to everyone. As a general rule, therefore, I do not accept the decision to terminate at face value.

Natalie A. was an 81-year-old woman, referred for therapy after a suicide attempt. She responded well to therapy, and after 3 months said she wanted to discontinue. The therapist asked for further information. She had no further symptoms or suicidal thoughts, she said. She then talked of her loneliness for the past 3 years following her husband's death, a low-level feeling of complete hopelessness, and a conviction that there would never be any pleasure or meaning in her life.

We arranged for a family session with her children, which confirmed her withdrawal and sadness, and she agreed to continue therapy. Very striking was the cheerfulness with which she left the session, which continued throughout the remaining treatment.

The desire to terminate, expressed by Mrs. A., represented, in part, a testing of the therapist, based upon many experiences of being let down. Had the termination been agreed upon, it would have confirmed her conviction that the therapist did not care. She would have, at best, continued with her empty, unhappy, meaningless lifestyle. Instead, there was a leap forward.

The difficult or unresponsive suicidal patient is similar to many of the patients described by Langsley, Kaplan et al., (1968) in their ground-breaking study of family crisis intervention as an alternative to hospitalization. They found that family crisis intervention was as effective and sometimes more so than admission to the hospital. In addition, those treated with outpatient crisis intervention required less hospitalization when future decompensation did occur.

Hospitalization, however, is sometimes necessary and desirable. However, as mentioned earlier, both hospitalization and discharge from the hospital must also be considered as a crisis and must be dealt with through crisis intervention. Otherwise the results can be deadly.

Bernard T., a 67-year-old polio victim on crutches, was hospitalized for a paranoid psychosis. The patient was a remarkably difficult man who "rejected" his therapist and spent most of the time demanding that he be discharged. When his therapist went on vacation, the staff did discharge him, without prior discussion with the therapist, but to the great relief of ward personnel. Upon discharge he was assigned to an overworked staff therapist in the mental hygiene clinic, who squeezed the patient into his schedule but did an incomplete evaluation. Two weeks later the patient committed suicide.

This case suggests how the NTR may be inseparable at times from an NCR (negative countertransference reaction). In a subsequent meeting on the ward, the therapist, nurses, and other staff members reviewed the subtle cues which indicated how important this ward therapist had been to this patient. The cues had been overlooked because of the negative reactions provoked by the patient.

The unacknowledged importance of the relationship to the suicidal patient can also be underestimated in outpatient therapy.

Karen C., age 67, had a history of psychotic breaks and suicidal behavior. She was in no serious distress and had always refused medication, but she and her husband agreed that she would benefit from a supportive relationship. She was seen for four sessions over 2 months and did extremely well. The therapist changed the fifth session to another date because of a conflict in his schedule.

The day before that scheduled meeting the patient phoned in a highly decompensated state, verbalizing delusional and deeply depressive ideas of worthlessness. The therapist immediately arranged to see her that day. At the meeting she continued her acutely disturbed verbalizations, while denying any relationship between her condition and the therapist. "I'm not angry at you because I know you had to change the time." However, the unmistakable message at a covert level was the statement, "See what happens when I let my defenses down? I trusted you and you showed me how wrong I was."

The implications of such examples are very clear. Never underestimate the importance of the relationship with a potentially suicidal person, no matter how it may appear on the surface, never neglect the contribution of the therapist as well as the patient to the NTR, and never give up on a patient, since lapses and mistakes in treatment are inevitable. They can be redeemed if, as Maltsberger and Buie (1974) emphasized, the therapist does not reject or abandon the patient. Labeling patients as untreatable, or shipping them off to state hospitals are forms of rejection and abandonment.

Correction of such errors is more easily accomplished when the therapist realizes that the NTR is inevitable. It is a predictable if paradoxical outcome of success in treatment, for reasons having to do with the family's perceived threat to its homeostatic equilibrium. Successful treatment of the suicidal patient is accomplished through a series of advances, followed by crises and seeming setbacks. Although the stress upon the therapist can be extreme, a setback is a problem to be dealt with and not a communication of failure by the therapist or the lack of treatability of the patient.

Combined with empathy, the CTR becomes a valued and constructive part of the treatment and a major ingredient in overcoming the NTR and other obstacles. The recognition that no elderly person becomes seriously suicidal without good, or should I say, terrible, reasons, and the expression of that understanding to the patient, is in itself therapeutic. The reasons arise out of experiences of great pain, which are brought into the therapy sessions.

The negative countertransference reaction leads some therapists to react with stress and tell the patient to stop what they are doing, in order for the therapist to feel better. Many therapists have ordered their suicidal patients not to talk about suicide. These therapists are the ones whose own pain has prevented a proper empathy.

Treatment is based upon the assets of the suicidal elderly and their forces for recovery. Elderly patients and their families possess a special wisdom regarding their strengths and weaknesses, and the measures they must take to survive. They often know more about that they need than the therapist, which is why the therapist can stop blaming or advising and begin listening.

Patients may terminate too soon or continue in therapy too long because of a too positive as well as a negative countertransference in the therapist. Some patients remain in treatment after therapy has accomplished all it has set out to do.

> Alice H., age 68, made a major, almost fatal suicide attempt. She recovered quickly, both physically and emotionally. However, she remained in therapy for 2 years after she was optimally well-functioning and free of her presenting symptoms. She was a good role model, a positive example to other group members, or so the therapist told himself.

Therapists often enjoy the company of such patients, especially with a caseload of predominantly borderline and psychotic patients.

Side taking, which can complicate and even undermine psychotherapy, is a combination of a positive countertransference towards one person combined with a negative or ambivalent countertransference towards others.

> Sadie and Jack L. entered therapy because of marital conflicts. She was 70, well-educated and American born. He was 80, uneducated, a retired working man with a foreign accent, born in a small town in Poland. He was also exhibiting signs of early dementia. The therapist's side taking assumed the form of "protecting" Mr. L., because Mrs. L. took advantage of her superior intelligence, education, and competence. As a result of the therapist's countertransference, the couple discontinued treatment prematurely.

Such examples emphasize that all therapists who treat suicidal and difficult patients need continued supervision or consultation, even those who are experienced.

Countertransference reactions also occur in professionals who are not engaged in psychotherapy.

> The psychotherapist of 85-year-old Harriet S. contacted her family doctor for information about her medical status. The doctor confided that Mrs. S.'s two sons were terrible people, and that the therapist should have nothing to do with them. He had never seen these sons, but Mrs. S. had told him how bad they were; they were completely neglectful and never came to see her.
>
> When the therapist insisted on a family meeting, Mrs. S. said her sons would not come. However, they not only came but they were eager to do so and wanted to improve their relationship. During the family interview the picture that emerged was dramatically different from that described by the family doctor. In actuality, one son visited Mrs. S. twice a week. The other maintained frequent telephone contacts. They both took her out on her birthday and Mother's Day for her favorite meal, a lobster shore dinner. They also picked her up and drove her to their homes on various other holidays and family functions, and were constantly available to help her maintain her home.

The side taking by the family doctor was a negative countertransference towards people not seen, a frequent phenomenon which occurs more often than is realized. It was benign in this case because it offered Mrs. S. the feeling that someone was on her side. It was undesirable, however, because it helped maintain an untenable status quo which increased her depression and led to somatic delusions and suicidal ideation.

Another form of countertransference involves the myth of exclusiveness, the belief that relationships are all or none, and that to form an intimate attachment to a new person means that the old relationships are destroyed. This false belief has been the basis of many difficulties in psychotherapy as well as in families. The patient may feel disloyal to his family if he forms a relationship with the therapist; while the therapist may perceive herself or himself in an adversarial position with the family.

The therapist may also be seduced by this myth of exclusiveness, seeing himself or herself as the replacement for the family. As one therapist declared, "More often than not, one finds that the only one who cares about the patient is the therapist" (Marks, 1985, p. 103). Such attitudes are a prescription for disaster when applied to the suicidal, unless the doctor–patient relationship is used to encourage a wider social cohesion. Berman and Jobes, for example, note that "The therapist is the primary support in the suicidal patient's life." However, they did not describe the therapist as in opposition to or as a replacement for others. They continue: "It is one of the therapist's primary responsibilities to recognize the power of his or her role and function for patients, and to use that power to broaden the patient's attachments beyond the therapist's office" (1991, p. 200).

The observations made in this book are based upon the view that transference and countertransference form an inseparable unit. Countertransference is not an impediment to be eliminated; rather it is one of the most valuable constituents of progress in therapy. One of the major signs of a successful countertransference is a quality of felt relatedness by the therapist towards the patient in which empathy and acceptance play significant roles.

The nature of the therapeutic relationship is not necessarily related to the severity of the patient's emotional disturbance.

Milton N. was a very paranoid and delusional black man in his middle 70's. Our relationship was very positive and we formed a working therapeutic alliance. The very openness of his delusions, his expressed awareness and yet acceptance of our ethnic and racial differences, and his willingness to share his current and past experiences played a major part.

At least 80% of my therapeutic relationships with suicidal persons have been preponderantly positive. There were several cases where my reactions were mixed, but few where they were predominantly negative. Related to the positive nature of the experience of treating the suicidal elderly is the responsiveness of most patients, their appreciation of being understood and listened to, and the untapped resources they bring to the treatment process.

The majority of elderly suicidal patients who recover and continue to do well make much use of denial. I accept their defenses and usually do not challenge or undermine them. However, I do intervene when their defenses or behaviors interfere with the major developmental tasks of aging. For example, with due consideration for the bereavement process and a willingness to go at the pace set by the patient, I pursue the painful processes of mourning. When I collude with the patient or family in avoiding the grief process, it is time to examine my countertransference.

The Management of Stress in the Therapist

The most important countertransference area of all is the stress aroused in the therapist and the aforementioned turmoil of distressing emotions, with a resulting depletion of resources and danger of burnout. Hopelessness in the therapist can then arise, often unrecognized as a problem but rationalized as a realistic appraisal of the patient's condition.

While a positive countertransference is the rule with the great majority of elderly suicidal patients, into each relationship some stress must fall, or else it is not a good relationship, and a successful resolution of the suicidal crisis is unlikely. Therefore, an awareness and understanding of the negative countertransference is essential. Suicidal persons are not only confronted with intense pain and distress, but the therapist must contact that very pain.

The following is a summary of some measures for actively dealing with the difficulties and stress of treatment.

1. A good, available professional support system, no matter how well trained and experienced the therapist. That means competent supervision and consultation. The proper selection of such supports must be considered. As Strean (1991) pointed out, there may also be a CTR in a supervisor, which can interfere with treatment. With suicidal patients, that can lead to undesirable and even dangerous consequences. Not everyone is qualified to supervise therapists who are treating the suicidal. Make sure,

therefore, that the consultant knows his suicide prevention business. Also valuable is the organization of peer supervision groups and continuous case seminars for those seeing suicidal patients.

2. A good personal support system. The therapist is not isolated, but instead turns to family, friends, and his more intimate network.

3. An alertness to one's own personal pressures and crises. Treatment of the suicidal cannot succeed when the therapist is in a state of crisis. The result is burnout in the self and ineffectiveness as a healer.

4. The cultivation of a sense of humor, which usually includes a healthy dose of humility. You do not have to be the expert. You can be the pupil as well as the teacher, and open to learning from all people.

5. The spiritual side of life has been too often disregarded by professionals. A meaningful philosophy of life, whether religious or secular, often arises intrinsically through working with people who have suffered deeply. It can be a source of strength, solace, and stress reduction.

6. Have fun. Take time out and time off; cultivate a relaxing lifestyle; increase your social life, spend more time with your family and go out more.

7. Respect your countertransference. Your reactions to hate, anger, guilt, fear, and anxiety are to be accepted as meaningful communications, not rejected and pushed away merely as problems in the therapist.

8. Expect the negative therapeutic reaction and do not react with a negative countertransference reaction.

9. Cultivate the ability to tolerate and respond effectively to the manipulations and raw affects of the suicidal person and family. Have a benign reaction to double bind situations, where whatever the therapist does is "wrong" or "bad," and a trap.

10. Acquire knowledge and skills, see many suicidal persons, and cultivate a professional flexibility. For example, it may be necessary to suspend analytic techniques or, indeed, techniques in general, and to respond intuitively to the requirements of the moment.

11. Avoid overidentification, and distrust rescue fantasies. Be human, but maintain your professional role.

12. Avoid overcommitment. Do not accept a suicidal patient when your schedule is full.

13. Above all, cultivate self-understanding, so that one's life tasks en-
hance and contribute to but do not interfere with effective treatment and suicide prevention. Self-examination is essential, but
may require help. It has been criticized in the humorous saying,
"Self-analysis is impossible because the countertransference gets
in the way" (Strean, 1991, p. 404).

Strean also pointed out that CTR problems exist for the most experienced analyst as well as the neophyte. Therefore, the one person the
therapist must work on most intensively for stress management and understanding is the self. Nevertheless, this cannot be accomplished alone,
even for those of us who are experienced and are the consultants and
therapists for others. It is the countertransference that propels the therapist into treatment for him or herself, to deal with the turmoil that has
been generated.

Suicide itself can be looked at as a stress reaction, the end result of all
the vicissitudes summarized in the chapters on individual and family
recognition, assessment, and therapy. More risk factors are present in
the elderly than in other groups. The availability of the family and others reduces the stress and provides suicidal people with the realization
that they are loved, even when they are old.

HEALING AND A POSITIVE ATTITUDE

A positive attitude towards the patient and family occurs through a
combination of intrinsic qualities in the self of the therapist and the effects of training and experience. The therapist's commitment, warmth,
and acceptance are part of this attitude. The therapist does not blame or
criticize the patient or family. These positive features are all potentially
life saving.

The attitude of others as well as one's own attitudes have an influence
upon mental and emotional disturbances and upon such behavior as
suicide. Sher, Baucom, and Larus (1990) and Hooley (1986) have presented research evidence to that effect. Sher and her colleagues noted
that "negative communication patterns appear to be of importance in
the lives of both depressed and maritally distressed individuals. For example, depressed persons returning home after hospitalization have a
greater chance of a relapse with relatives who are high in expressed
emotion or EE. Expressed emotion includes the amount of criticism and
hostility regarding the patient" (p. 64).

One recommendation is for the use of the "corrective emotional experience," as described by Alexander and French (1945). As usual, the therapist remains alert to the negative therapeutic reaction, which is likely to follow success. The corrective experience would be a relationship that is high in positive regard and communication and low in criticism and hostility. The application of the corrective experience to the family is described in the following chapter.

5

Family Therapy with the Suicidal Elderly

> An old farmhand on a family estate was an expert with the whip, and delighted to show his prowess. One afternoon he gave a demonstration to a group of guests, skillfully striking a blossom from a daisy, and then hitting a fly in midair. A guest then pointed to a hornet's nest, but the old man shook his head. "A blossom is a blossom and a fly is a fly," he said and added wisely, "but a hornet's nest—that's an organization."
>
> —*The Folk Wisdom of Jokes*

THE FAMILY AS A POSITIVE RESOURCE

The positive aspects of family relationships are intuitively grasped, better perhaps by artists and novelists than the scientific community. For example, an affectionate tribute to the family was written by Elie Wiesel (1990), who described why the musical play, "The Rothschilds" has been such a continuing success.

"First," he says, "the family. It remains united, close-knit, sustained by a common purpose. Even when it is scattered geographically, it will not permit itself to be torn apart. The sons quarrel now and then about tactics, but even when they clash it is to protect the family—by which they themselves are protected—not to break it down."

Then, continues Wiesel, there is the mother. "Her sons show her respect and affection sometimes going so far as to ask her advice on

96

business matters." What? Portray a Jewish mother and not make fun of her? Love a Jewish mother without being ridiculed? Apparently you can. "The most moving aspect of this play comes when we realize that we have been present at a true celebration of the family, any family, irrespective of its ethnic origins" (p. 6).

Elie Wiesel intuitively recognized that the family is a system which at its best is based upon love without social narrowing and loyalty without self-impoverishment. The ideal family is united, close knit, sustained by a common purpose even when separated geographically. The members work hard to protect the family, which protects them. The children protect the parents and do not derogate or humiliate them.

These statements by Wiesel are prescriptions for family cohesion that permit and facilitate individuation and growth. The family that can work together is a powerful force ready to help any of its members in need and to stick by those in crisis. The strength of the family is in its cohesiveness and loyalty.

I have found that the family involved in a suicidal state is also a potential treasure, the foundation of cure as well as of stress. These strengths may even be present in families that are disorganized and falling apart. Elizabeth Swados (1991) whose own family was plagued by suicide and mental illness found a community of caring in young people struggling with the same family difficulties. While working on her play, *Runaways,* "I saw that many of the young cast members were chased by demons similar to mine" (p. 47). She saw that kids suffered and destroyed themselves to make mother and father stop fighting each other. They became sick or depressed to distract a parent from his or her despair. They ran away or committed crimes to take the heat off abusive or neglectful parents. "Kids were loyal and loving to the most awful characters simply because it was dictated by love" (p. 47).

William Styron (1990) was another writer who provided great insights into the nature of depression and despair. He believed that the support of his family helped prevent his suicide. He wrote with sympathy and love of his "long suffering wife . . . whose wisdom far exceeded that of Dr. Gold." Such support, he added, can prevent suicide.

Such reflections apply to life-saving and suicide preventing forces in the social and professional network outside the immediate family. Physicians such as Payne (1975) recognized that a doctor's wish for a suicidal patient to live has saved many lives. Similarly, Styron said that what he called the devotion of others "has prevented countless suicides."

Styron particularly singled out the support of a friend who kept telling Styron that suicide was "unacceptable." The attitude of this devoted friend, who had been severely suicidal himself, supports the recommendation for homogeneous therapy groups, where those who have been through the suicidal state are the most understanding and effective in helping someone who is actively suicidal. (See Chapter 6, on group psychotherapy.)

Anne Sexton, whose suicide was a loss to family and friends as well as the literary world, also described the family conflicts and rivalries that were related to her suicidal behavior. Difficulties were particularly intense between her and her mother. However, her mother also affirmed Sexton as a person and as a writer: "You have something to give—a word—The word . . . *you* are adult in your sense of decency" (Middlebrook, 1991, p. 47). Anne Sexton also recalled when she was younger, writing stories, and her mother reading one to a friend. In her therapy Anne Sexton recognized her own achievements "as strengths supported by this particular identification with her mother" (p. 49). She discovered, too, that her father was extremely proud of her. With suicidal people, the resources of pride, affirmation, and love inherent in the family organization are relied upon for healing and growth.

FAMILY TENSIONS AND SUICIDE

Consistent with Wiesel's celebration of the family, research has confirmed the family basis of the enjoyment of living among the elderly. Medley reported that "Satisfaction with family was found to make the greatest single impact on life satisfaction" (Medley, 1976, p. 448). Similar results were reported by McCulloch (1990).

However, not all families are constructive; some are destructive and, in even the best of families, periods of severe and distressing discord and conflict take place. The family is where the most intense and disruptive problems in living arise and are played out, and unlike the "Rothschild's," the play can be deadly. That may be particularly true of the family in which suicidal behavior occurs. It is in the family that suicidal messages are communicated most frequently.

The underlying origins of suicidal states are similar throughout the life span, but the overt reasons may differ at different ages. In my studies comparing the motives and precipitants of attempted suicide or ideation in younger and older suicidal persons, age differences were found. Younger persons were responding to such problems as the breaking up of a love affair and failure or strain in school and other activities. The older subjects were dealing with such issues as retirement, illness, and the deaths of loved ones (Richman, 1975).

However, there was much overlap between the younger and older groups, especially in the areas of illness and loss. The higher risk young persons were more similar in their precipitants and motives to the older suicidal ones. Most striking was the pervasiveness of family conflicts and dissension. These were apparent in 90 percent of the younger subjects and 70 percent of the older.

A major perennial question has been the choice of symptom. Why suicide or, in contrast, why not more adaptive and creative measures? There is no one answer that applies to all conditions. Suicide is a multi-determined act in which biological factors and various life events may play a part; but extensive clinical experience indicates that the family plays a major psychodynamic role in the choice of suicide. At the time of a suicidal act family conflicts are major factors, but the family is also a major factor in subsequent healing and growth. Recognition of the positive potentials of the family is a major tenet of family therapy. For example, Minuchin (1974) saw "the family as the matrix of healing" (p. 116). The implications for treatment are far reaching. "In effect, I turn other family members into my cotherapists making of the larger unit the matrix for healing" (p. 121).

Such family support and understanding may be overlooked by investigators who engage in a single-minded search for what went wrong. That is not true in well-conducted family therapy sessions with suicidal patients, where good feelings and good humor are frequent, especially at the end of a session. Many colleagues, whose offices are near mine, have commented on how much laughter and lively conversation they hear. At the time of the suicidal crisis, however, both the family and the suicidal member are trapped in a negative condition which appears hopeless, with no way out. Although examples of "malevolent" families may be seen, they are more often in need of help to become unstuck and to utilize their resources.

The family is both part of society yet separate from the outside world. Just as the individual cannot be understood outside his or her context, the family cannot be understood outside of the larger society. Conflicts between the suicidal individual and the family usually involve institutions within this larger society. The closed family system is a maladaptive attempt to deal with disturbed family roles and relationships. The opening up of this closed system is one of the most helpful results of family therapy for both the suicidal person and loved ones.

This chapter deals with the family aspect of the suicidal state. Relevant descriptions of family dynamics and treatment have been presented throughout this book because they are so intrinsic to the healing relationship in all therapy. What follows is an integrated and unified outline of the family aspects.

FROM SEPARATION INTOLERANCE TO CRISIS INTOLERANCE

At the time of a suicidal crisis, the family possesses certain identifiable features, some chronic and based upon enduring traits and experiences, and others more acute and situational. They have been touched upon in Chapter 1, on Recognition. The nature of the family at the time of a suicidal attempt is summarized in Table 5.1.

Table 1.1 in Chapter 1 presented the characteristics of an individual at the time of a suicidal state, as reflected in the demographic, epidemiological, and clinical recognition signs. Chapter 2 on assessment described the combined use of Tables 1.1 and 5.1 as a check list of suicidal risk factors.

A comparison between Table 5.1 and 1.1 suggests a dramatic correspondence between the *family* at the time of a suicidal state in one of its members, and the *individual* tensions and other danger signs. I have previously suggested that this correspondence represents an isomorphism between the self and the family, the inner structure and outer organization. The family is not always in such a troubled state, but it is at the time of a suicidal episode in one of its members. Given sufficient stress and provocation, virtually all families are vulnerable.

The accumulation of individual signs combined with family indicators translates into feelings of hopelessness, for which death becomes the symbol. Indeed, words like "death," "die," and "kill" are frequent in the family interviews with suicidal people, more than in the families of other groups. The specific forms the family characteristics assume in the suicidal elderly overlap with but differ in some respects from their younger counterparts. The relevant family characteristics in the elderly include the following.

Intolerance For Separation

Separation occupies a pivotal position in the development and outcome of a suicidal state. Because of the family history and the attendant anxiety, separation has become equated with death in the unconscious of the family members, and therefore an extraordinarily painful experience.

Table 5.1
Characteristics of Families with a Suicidal Member[1]

I. An inability to accept necessary change
  a. an intolerance for separation
  b. an association of change with separation
  c. an association of development with separation
  d. an association of separation with death
  e. a symbiosis without empathy
  f. a clinging to early attachments at the expense of later ones
  g. an inability to mourn

II. Role and interpersonal conflicts, failures, and fixations
  a. an intolerance for failure
  b. a fear of success
  c. a fusion of self and social roles

III. A disturbed family structure
  a. a closed family system
  b. an association of the open family with loss
  c. a prohibition against intimacy outside the family
  d. an isolation of the potentially suicidal person within the family
  e. fragility of a key family member

IV. Unbalanced or one-sided intrafamilial relationships
  a. a specific kind of scapegoating
  b. double binding relationships
  c. sadomasochistic relationships
  d. ambivalent relationships
  e. an association of relationships outside the home with loss

V. Affective difficulties
  a. a one-sided pattern of aggression
  b. an association of aggression with death
  c. a family depression
  d. an association of autonomous emotions with separation

VI. Transactional difficulties
  a. communication disturbances
  b. an excessive secretiveness
  c. open communication associated with danger

VII. An intolerance for crises
  a. an association of crisis with separation
  b. an association of crisis with preventing separation

[1]Adapted From Richman, J. (1986) *Family Therapy For Suicidal People*. New York: Springer Publishing Co.

With age there is inevitably a greater number of losses of all kinds, as well as a greater closeness to one's own death. The vicissitudes of aging sometimes bother younger people more than the elderly, with a resulting disruption of relationships. The association of old people with loss makes them almost taboo to family members who are particularly fearful of separation and death. The problem is not only loss and death but the inability of the family to be caring and available.

Anna C. at age 80 had coped with the deaths of her parents, her only sister, a large number of uncles and aunts, most of the friends she had known during her life, and finally her husband. That was the last straw and she fell into a deep despair. However, there was a "ripple effect" following the death of her husband, in that the loss led to myriad other losses. Her son, her daughter and their families, for example, all avoided her. Feeling completely alone, Mrs. C. made a major suicide attempt from which she only accidentally survived.

Separation or loss can never in itself be an explanation for suicide except in terms of an entire social system or family organization which cannot deal with the problem. It is not the losses but their meaning, how they are handled, and the subsequent events that are vital. Above all, the presence and availability of support systems, and especially the family, makes the difference in the onset and recovery from a suicidal state.

Suicide becomes an issue when the individual, family members, and others in the social network all react traumatically to the combination of depression, bereavement, and loss, with the resulting crisis escalating the grief and despair. Most elderly persons can come to terms with these losses without becoming suicidal. What then are the selective factors?

One such factor is depression in the suicidal individual, which follows or is exacerbated following a loss. There is a significant cognitive factor in depression as Beck and his associates (1979) have convincingly demonstrated. In the suicidal elderly there is a perception of the past, present, and future as consisting only of separation and loss. The depressed old person thinks, "Who needs it?" Recognition of the depression by family members or others may go a long way towards preventing suicide.

Another factor is the effort to preserve an untenable status quo, which one observer defined as "the name of the mess that we are all in." Why do people cling to such a mess? In fact, as previously discussed, people are trying to prevent separation and think they can do so be maintaining the status quo.

There is also a significant interpersonal component involved in suicide, as demonstrated by Klerman et al. (1984). Both the interpersonal and the individual components are part of the person's social and family system. As we saw in the case of "Anne C.," suicide is most likely to become an issue when family members and others in the social network are not able to be supportive. Instead, they react traumatically to expressions of loss and depression by the vulnerable individual. The result is a crisis based upon escalating grief and despair.

Younger people are less subject to irrevocable losses. In addition, there is a difference between the separation dynamics of the older and younger suicidal person. Youth is struggling for autonomy while the family is striving to maintain a state of enmeshment. Age is striving for attachment, while the other family members are often trying to separate from them. Nevertheless, in one form or another, separation is the main impetus behind the suicidal state at all ages.

Separation was once considered *the* goal of development and the primary task of growing up, while attachment was ignored or criticized. As Freud said, "The detachment of the child from his parents is thus a task that cannot be evaded if the young individual's social fitness is not to be endangered" (1957, p. 48). There are times and situations, however, where detachment without attachment is neither desirable nor a sign of growth.

> When George P. became suicidal at age 75 and his wife became severely depressed, their son and his family distanced themselves both literally and emotionally. They moved to another part of the country, stopped visiting, and especially tried to keep the grandchildren from becoming "upset" by seeing their grandparents. The grandparents both committed suicide. One year later, the family was seen, because the 40-year-old son was suicidal, and the grandson had become a severe school and behavior problem.

In all cases of suicide pacts or murder-suicides with which I am familiar, key family figures had distanced themselves. They often did not consciously realize that they did so, but they had become unavailable and unsupporting.

Such removal is one of the factors in social isolation which is such a significant risk factor for suicide. Attachment is not only a phase of the infant-mother relationship that ends with childhood. Rather, it is an enduring process that continues throughout adult life in the development of intimacy and later, of generativity.

The need of the younger generation to separate from the older as part of their own growth striving cannot be used as a rationale for abandonment, isolation or, as is happening increasingly in our society, the approval of elderly suicide. Attachment is an intrinsic aspect of healthy separation. The development of an autonomous self and the pursuit of activity and competence cannot take place through the rejection of attachment.

The Symbiotic Nature Of The Family System

The term *symbiosis* has been the focus of various emotional and value judgments, which has enriched its meanings and connotations. In biology the term refers to the "association of two different organisms which live attached to each other, or one as a tenant of the other, and contribute to each other's support" (Oxford Universal Dictionary Abridged, 1955, p. 2108). In psychoanalysis, symbiosis is defined in similar terms as "the interdependent condition of the human infant and its mother. The term . . . draws attention to the need each has for the other and the different gratification each gives to and gets from the other" (Moore & Fine, 1990, p. 190).

Some psychologists tended to be more pejorative and mean spirited. English and English (1958), for example, defined symbiosis as "a condition in which a person depends upon others, not for cooperative mutual support and affection but for exploitation and the satisfaction of neurotic needs: for example, the sadistic wit dependent upon his stooge. The stooge equally depends upon the wit—perhaps financially. Both 'profit,' but the 'profit' is neurotic" (p. 538).

Since the contributions of Margaret Mahler to developmental theory, symbiosis has been more thoroughly understood as a normal phase of infant development in which the self and the mother are merged or fused. Development proceeds from symbiosis, to separation-individuation, on the road to individual autonomy.

Boss and her colleagues (1990) presented the valuable concept of family boundaries from which one is included or extruded. She also presents the presence of ambiguous, labile or unstable boundaries. Her work is consistent with my concept of symbiosis in the family as polarized into two aspects, overinclusion and exclusion or detachment. Both are present, often represented by different individuals, but all are part of the symbiosis. For example, a symbiotic dyad will be overinclusive and merged while a third essential person will be detached.

The exclusion of children from family boundaries is seen in Sabbath's (1969) "expendable child." In the elderly it often appears as social isolation. Characteristic of symbiosis, in other words, is the polarization between extremes of fusion and extrusion. The two extremes may exist simultaneously through the assignment of different roles in the family.

Symbiosis and the Family

The family context of a disturbed symbiosis has been noted almost from the beginning. Mahler (1968) found that self destructive activity was prominent during the symbiotic phase when combined with a disturbed mother-child relationship. For development to be resumed, the needs of the mother had to be recognized, understood, and responded to before the child with a symbiotic psychosis could be treated successfully.

> For example, Mahler (1968) described a self-destructive child with a symbiotic psychosis, whom she called Violet, who was seen with her mother in a therapeutic nursery. The staff noticed that during feeding time Violet's mother would clandestinely steal food from her daughter's plate. It was not until they fed the mother together with the daughter that Violet began to improve.

The story of Violet and her mother is an example of good family therapy. It worked because neither Violet nor her mother were blamed or else singled out through a diagnosis, as is typical of the medical model. Instead, both Violet and her mother were provided with mothering by feeding them both. The importance of the therapist as a good mother figure will be discussed further in this chapter.

The oral needs behind symbiosis stand out. In the notes he kept on the treatment of the "Wolf-Man," Freud (1955) described how the patient came to see him, tired and hungry, and Freud fed him. I believe that Freud was in touch with his patient's needs to be comforted and fed. In treating the suicidal elderly, even with insight-oriented psychotherapy, the availability of food is often present, with the same intuitive, empathic awareness of the eternal, deep-seated needs for mothering. It is relevant in terms of a symbiotic family pattern that both the sister and later the wife of the Wolf-Man committed suicide (The Wolf-Man, 1971). (His autobiography published in 1971, maintaining his anonymity under the name of "The Wolf-Man.")

In families that are poorly differentiated, symbiosis is experienced as essential, and efforts at individuation in one of its members as a threat to the family system. The result is a series of destructive events and interactions designed to bring the person who is trying to individuate back to the customary symbiotic pattern. That process is behind the statement of Litman and Tabachnick (1968) that suicide is based upon a regression to the separation-individuation stage of development.

Suicidal behavior or psychotic breaks during psychotherapy often occur because of premature efforts by the therapist to undermine a symbiotic system and force individuation before the family is ready. Acceptance of the symbiosis during therapy and letting the family go at its own pace are more effective steps towards individuation. The problem in suicide is not only separation, but the wish to merge, to become one with the person who is lost or unavailable.

In the vulnerable elderly the loss or threatened loss of the symbiotic other is especially poignant after years of attachment. The biblical commandment for a man and a woman to leave their parents and become one flesh does not occur overnight or with the voicing of the marriage vows. The increased suicidal risk among widowers occurs in the loss of close relationships where years of being together have made that biblical injunction a reality.

The Nature of Suicide Pacts

In all cases, suicide pact ideations are communications. They are expressions of pain and despair, calling for assessment, intervention, and treatment. In my elderly suicidal patients who were married, suicide pact ideation was a frequent occurrence. Treatment was consistently successful.

The longer the relationship and the stronger the attachment, the greater the pain when that attachment is threatened. Thoughts of suicide pacts then arise with a greater frequency than is generally realized. That applies whether the suicides are dyadic, such as between a husband and wife, or a homosexual couple in which one or both has AIDS, or communal, as in the mass murder-suicides in Guyana. It was there that the Reverend Jim Jones made the classic symbiotic statement that whatever happens to one of us happens to all of us. He said this shortly after the death of his mother. His dying words were, "Mother, mother, mother, mother, mother, mother, mother!" (Richman, 1979, p. 5).

Suicide pact ideation can also cut across generations in vulnerable families:

> Elizabeth Swados described how after her brother, Lincoln, attempted suicide, her mother went into shock. "She told many people in different ways that she wanted to go get my brother, and lock herself and him in a garage with the car running" (Swados, 1991, p. 102).

His mother's hopelessness and suicidal pact ideation were communications that the family was faced with a problem that appeared insoluble. This was a crisis and therefore also an opportunity. Lincoln was damaged both physically and mentally and lived in a different town, but such barriers can be overcome. His mother's shock reaction was the call for crisis intervention and family therapy.

However, few people know that the pain and hopelessness behind suicide pacts can be relieved. Instead, there is a movement in the popular media to encourage such suicides among the elderly rather than to relieve the pain. Examples include a television segment from *60 Minutes* called "Till Death do us Part," and "The Liberation of Lolly and Gronky," in *Life Magazine* (Fadiman, 1986).

My criticism of these presentations has been given in more detail elsewhere (Richman, 1990). Rather than considering or providing alternatives, these essays presented suicide pacts as *the* solution to problems of illness and disability in the elderly. However, suicide pact ideation can more fruitfully be seen as the communication of a problem in the couple and family system that needs resolution.

Unfinished Family Business

The staying power of the primary family relationship is a dominant feature of families with a suicidal member. Close family ties are not a problem, as I have stated earlier (Richman, 1986), except when three conditions are present. First, the early attachments interfere with the development of later ones. Healthy early relationships, in contrast, facilitate the formation of mature later relationships.

Second is the "myth of exclusiveness." In this myth the presence of an intimate new relationship is falsely believed to mean the ending or "breaking off" of a significant early relationship. While the belief may be false, it is part of the family system and can become a self-fulfilling prophecy. The dominance of this myth of exclusiveness is found even into great old age.

Third, when an elderly person becomes suicidal, submerged early relationships surface in the form of a re-arousal of earlier family and parent–child relationships. The unresolved childhood conflicts and resentments are activated and played out once again. Early conflicts are persistent. They begin in childhood, continuing when the "children" are middle-aged and the parents elderly. An analysis of humor has found a similar pattern, of parent–child relationships that remain remarkably unchanging as the protagonists age.

There is the story of the person who returned from school crying: "I don't want to go to school anymore," he told his father. "The teachers hate me, the pupils hate me, even the superintendent hates me." His father said sternly, "You have to go and that's all there is to it. Besides, you're 51 years old and the principal."

Impediments to the Mourning Process

Unresolved grief can be the major stumbling block to growth and well-being, not only in individuals, but in the family. Virtually every anecdote and case history in this book involves incomplete mourning. It is the older person who often responds appropriately to a loss, but is responded to inappropriately by others. An elderly and potentially suicidal person is often the recipient of the family's inability to deal with a death, especially when the deceased is the focus of secretiveness and other communication disturbances:

> When Mrs. T.'s daughter died, she had a need to share her feelings of loss and memories of her daughter. However, she had been kept in the dark about the true circumstances of the death, which was related to illicit activities by the daughter which led to her demise. As a result, the grandchildren reacted with distress and anger toward Mrs. T. As one of them confided to a doctor after Mrs. T.'s suicide attempt, "It was 2 months after my mother had died, and grandma still wanted to talk about her!"

The treatment of Mrs. T. and her family will be described later in this chapter.

A Closed Family System

The closed family system refers to a family that sees the world outside as an inimical force which threatens the survival of the family's system of values, roles, and behavior. Consequently, the family seals itself off, often in a covert manner, often while maintaining the appearance of contact and interaction with the outside world:

> Herman and Gladys F. were both in their mid-70's, seemingly content and socially active in their retirement community. No one knew that Herman was massively depressed and Gladys was overwhelmed with anxiety. He refused medical or any other treatment, but regularly took the Valium which the family doctor has prescribed for her.

In addition, no one knew that the only meaningful contact was with their daughter, who lived in another state but visited once a year at Christmas. As fate would have it, while the emotional distress of Mr. and Mrs. F. was escalating, their daughter was faced with a dilemma. Her cat was having kittens, and she felt that she could not leave her at such a time. She cancelled her usual visit. Two days later Herman F. murdered Gladys and killed himself.

The couple in this sad case could have been successfully treated. The closed family consistently is involved in family relationships and contacts that have been disrupted. The secretiveness and indirect forms of communication and the "role narcissism" are prominent forces behind the closing off.

The closed family is one of the more serious danger signs. The members are represented in the "help rejectors," discussed in Chapter 1, and "the difficult patient," touched upon in Chapter 4. Such recalcitrant patients are often acting out the concealed dynamics of the closed family, which sees the health system as an enemy, threatening to force a separation the family is unready for and feels it must resist:

Swados described the traumatic reaction of her family when the high school advised that her mentally ill brother, Lincoln, be sent away to a special school for the emotionally disturbed. Evidently, their separation anxiety was aroused. "A dismal anxious mood settled in the household. Lincoln kept entirely to his room. My mother went to bed" (Swados, 1991, p. 18).

Such descriptions must be listened to. They reinforce the necessity of broadening the definition of the patient in such cases to include the key family members and significant others.

The closed and open family can be defined in terms of the degree of adaptation to the outside world and flexibility in response to changing conditions. Adaptability is characterized by an acceptance of change or development. The maladaptive family is characterized by rigidity and efforts to prevent change. The basis for such constriction of their life space is the association of change with the threat of separation and loss and the outside world forcing such changes.

The closed family assumes various forms. In elderly couples where one committed suicide, Bock and Webber (1972) found much marital isolation. Like Herman and Gladys F., these couples walled themselves off from others, much like the social isolation associated with suicides in general.

There is a similar phenomenon which might be called "dyadic isolation," found in people who meet and possess the same suicidogenic dynamics. They form a closed unit, two against the world. For example, when two suicidal people get together, they are likely to instigate each other to suicidal acts.

However, when three or more suicidal people get together, they tend to reinforce each other's healing, rescuing, and life-enhancing forces. In other words, the more open the system and the more others are allowed in, the more likely that the person would bend under stress and adversity rather than break. This pattern and its modification is considered in more detail in the chapter on group therapy.

Role Development Versus Stagnation

The family is the place where roles, relationships, and fundamental attitudes towards the self and others are learned in childhood and maintained and reinforced throughout life. Roles develop, they change, are outgrown, and some are discarded with age.

A major problem is a developmental lag, seen as a clinging to earlier roles. To accept changes, even desirable ones, past developmental roles must be mourned. Many people, however, fear that they will lose more than they will gain by giving up the past. The results can sometimes be unfortunate:

> David B., age 83, and Martha B., age 78, had a remarkably stable lifestyle throughout their 55 years of marriage. He worked and took care of the home, both financially and physically. He was an accomplished carpenter and electrician who kept the home in working order and who took care of all the bills. Although they were childless, his wife did not work throughout the marriage, but she did cook and clean.
>
> Problems developed. David progressively did less and less in the house and neglected the bills, while Martha became increasingly distraught. However, she felt completely incapable of taking over any of the tasks that had been in David's province. One day, David made a serious suicide attempt and was hospitalized. The doctors eventually discovered that Mr. B. suffered from a progressive dementia that must have had an insidious onset at least 3 years before. Blind spots in recognizing his condition were based upon an effort to maintain the old roles when a change was required.
>
> Mr. and Mrs. B. entered into treatment. While Mr. B. was the identified patient, it was Mrs. B. who was in the greater distress. She was in a developmental crisis which perhaps should have taken place 50 years earlier in their marriage. In therapy she became less depressed and anxiety-ridden, more competent and self-sufficient. First, however, she had to mourn her role as a child-bride, unrealistic as it was. "Suddenly I'm old," she said, before taking over the tasks Mr. B. could no longer perform.

The changes that are necessitated with age rarely involve only one person:

> The problem is symbolically presented in a lighter vein, in the story of an elderly man who saw a little boy sitting at a curb, crying. "Why are you crying?" asked the man. "I am crying because I can't do what the big boys do," sobbed the little boy. So the old man sat down and cried too.

Both the young child and the old man lived under the spell of the cult of youth. Herodotus reports a story:

> Two youths, Klobis and Biton, were both distinguished for their remarkable strength and had won many a victory in the gymnastic games. Because oxen were missing, they pulled their mother, a priestess of Hera, in her chariot a great distance to the sanctuary of Argos. For this pious deed their mother prayed to the gods to reward them and, as the greatest boon they could grant, the gods allowed the two brothers to die in their sleep in the full strength of their youth (Naegele, 1965, p. 51).

The adoration and near-worship of such youth-oriented attitudes in our day can be understood, once again, as an expression of the ubiquitous developmental lag, an intrusion of pagan ideals where they do not belong in our age of the expanded life span. However, even in pagan times the mother of these young men may have thought that their deaths were a lousy reward for being such good sons.

The concept of "role narcissism" to suicidal behavior, as described by De Vos (1968) and applied to the role disturbances of families (Richman, 1986), is a noteworthy contribution. The family members are sensitive to how their social role is perceived by others, often a generalized "they." It is as though who they are depends upon how others judge them.

Older persons who are vulnerable to depression and suicidal states often react with shame to the loss of roles resulting from retirement and physical or mental decline. They therefore become increasingly withdrawn and depressed which, combined with other difficulties, may culminate in suicide.

The family basis of this attitude is well described by Swados. In the family, "everything had to be 'fine.' Appearance was everything. . . . Difficult children reflected inept parents" (1991, p. 4). In order to keep up appearances, a greater and greater secretiveness developed and a subtle closing off of the family from the outside world. A family cannot interact with other people or agencies when they perceive these figures as being primarily critical and judgmental. Nor can they enter into therapy.

Swados added that she was describing a family of the 1950s, but that the atmosphere is different in the 1990s. However, her description of how role narcissism led to the closed family in the 1950s corresponds with remarkable fidelity to families of the 1990s.

Role failure is a major component in the suicidal states of the elderly, but role success is also a danger because of the threat of separation it poses. Examples associated with suicide include the opposition of family members to new heterosexual relationships established by a widow or widower, or even new friendships.

The variety of role disturbances in the elderly contains a strong family component because a role assignment in one person is part of a pattern of roles. Therefore, a change in the role of one person in the family impacts on the roles of others. As seen in the case of David and Martha B., the interrelationship of roles becomes particularly evident in elderly couples when the active or dominant member becomes ill and the other must take over.

Roles change with age and roles are lost with age, often those considered vital to self-esteem and even to one's very identity. Such loss of roles is often based upon retirement, reduced income, fewer friends, decreased social opportunities, and the effects of illness. Not all role loss is based upon the family; it is part of a wider social situation.

But there are positive roles of the aged, such as their function as carriers of the traditions and history of the culture, sometimes dating back thousands of years. There is an analogous function in the family where the elderly can represent the past history, traditions, and experiences that shaped the family system.

And there are negative aspects of aging. The elderly also represent the dark side of the family's past, events that only become known after a suicide or some other death. The older parent or grandparent may also be the recipient of resentments around the unfinished tasks and unresolved conflicts of children and other members of the family. The elderly may be blamed for unfulfilled dreams and feelings of having been insufficiently loved or appreciated. In the family, the past is present and very much alive.

The elderly make their positive and negative contributions to the basic meaning of the family by what they are, not by what they do. The family and the social system that does not realize this symbolic role of the elderly, which lends meaning to history, are suffering a greater loss, with more serious implications for the future than realized. Nevertheless, as we shall see, roles cannot be differentiated from relationships and behavior.

The difficulties, complexities, and pain of role changes are very great. As with separation, the therapist does not prematurely press for role development and growth. That does not take place until both the suicidal person and the family are ready.

Disturbed Interpersonal Relationships

Loneliness, loss, and conflict can form a deadly combination. Suicide is associated with isolation, a constriction of the social and interpersonal field, and disturbances in the few relationships that are present. These are typical problems that occur with age, when the social system tends to shrink as friends and relatives die or move away. As Peck (1975) emphasized, one of the major tasks of successful aging is to maintain old friendships and family contacts and to replace those that are lost.

These social problems are best understood within a family context, no matter how remote they may appear. Conflicts between the family and the formation of independent outside relationships have been conceptualized as a reaction to the needs of young people to separate from the family. However, the family may object as strenuously to an older person acquiring new attachments, a severe problem for those most at risk of suicide.

The symbiotic family pattern is preserved by the isolation and exclusion of various members, but they are part of the family nevertheless, by virtue of their very isolation. New attachments, even in older persons who are ostensibly isolated and not part of the family, may be threatening to the relatives, intensifying their fear of change and loss.

Social relationships are strained in the suicidal by the prevalence of interpersonal discord and conflict. These typically assume the form of ambivalent and double binding relationships, scapegoating, and other unworkable transactions. In the elderly associated problems, such as retirement, physical decline, giving up driving, and other events, are involved in the decline in social contacts.

The decline also touches upon the persistence of the myth of exclusiveness into advanced old age and it highlights other family rules against the person forming intimate attachments outside the family, in order to preserve the older primary relationships:

May B. is a 70-year-old woman with a 25-year history of depressive episodes and suicide attempts. She lives with her 79-year-old brother and 40-year-old schizophrenic son. She and her brother regularly attended a senior center. They stopped, however, because he objected to what he described as her inappropriate behavior. During lunch she fed a man who was disabled by a stroke. Her brother said, "My sister should not associate with such low class people." He also said she might become too attached to such persons (and presumably leave him).

Mrs. B. was the depressed, suicidal, and nonfunctional patient, while her brother was successful and overfunctional. Nevertheless, she appeared much more appropriate and realistic. Together with her psychotic son, who often would not let them leave the house because of the dangers in the world outside, they all three contributed to a family system in trouble.

Affective Disturbances

As we have seen, family rules govern the expression and discharge of affects. One such rule is to avoid the expression of grief or other unpleasant feelings directly, because that would upset others. Feelings, however, have a life of their own and refuse to be denied. The resulting family conflicts can be most disruptive and lead to self-destruction. As a general rule, where suicide (or murder) becomes an issue, the task is to determine the area where separation is most threatened, because all else may be misleading:

> Sylvia G.'s husband died when she was 67. Her daughter told her not to talk about the deceased and stopped her visits. Mrs. G. felt angry and guilty over feeling angry. Her depression deepened, and as she became aware of her daughter's buried depression, she felt she was a burden who was harmful to the one she loved most. Mrs. G.'s open expression of grief and sadness was, in fact, deeply threatening to her daughter, who feared the consequences of opening the floodgates of her suppressed feelings.

Such strong but buried emotional reactions are derived most often from an upsurge of separation and death anxiety. These escalate when the family must deal with illness and death because mourning is so unbearably painful. A process is initiated leading to depression, rage, a state of undifferentiated turmoil, death wishes, and other intense and unbearable feelings, culminating in despair and hopelessness and finally a suicidal state.

Anger, rage, and death wishes are reactions to loss, separation, and incomplete mourning, but that does not make them any less deadly. They also perform defensive functions. They are used to replace grief and avoid the bereavement process. They are also used to avoid the compelling need to resolve old problems and heal old wounds. Since mourning is so intolerable to others, the one grieving becomes the recipient of messages that their behavior, and indeed their very existence, is harmful. By such means the crisis that follows a death escalates to deadly proportions:

> When Michael T.'s second wife died he became very angry at her children. When they came to his house to pay a condolence call, he ran into the kitchen and emerged holding a sharp knife and ordered them to leave. One of the sons grabbed the knife, cutting himself, and the other son beat up Mr. T. severely. The entire family, two sons and their wives, together with Mr. T., ended up in the emergency room.

This was a typical example of what Berne (1964) called "uproar." A skilled crisis intervention in the hospital might have helped avert the split that isolated Mr. T. from a potential support system. Crisis intervention can help maintain family cohesion and permit a more appropriate grief process. In the psychotherapy with Mr. T. that followed, he broke into uncontrollable sobs at any mention of his wife, but immediately changed that to rage at her sons. Nevertheless, he also expressed a willingness to attempt a reconciliation. The "children" (all in their fifties), however, refused any such efforts.

Emotional turmoil is prevalent at the time of a suicidal state. Such overwhelming affects and behaviors are behind the high perturbation level and unbearable psychological pain which was described by Shneidman (1985, 1988) as the foundation of all genuine suicidal acts, together with intense environmental stress.

High EE or "expressed emotion" is the most frequent pattern at the time of a suicidal state. In families with high EE, the members are critical, hostile, and overly involved with the person at risk. The term "EE" was first applied to schizophrenics, where it was observed that patients from families high in such characteristics were hospitalized more frequently, were less compliant with medication and other aspects of the treatment plans, and in general did less well than those from families who were low in EE. (It might be more accurate to call it negative EE, since overly involved families high in positive expressed emotions do not have such destructive results.)

The emotional state leading to suicide represents a disconfirmation of the self, of others, and of life. Fortunately, however, a great ambivalence is present beneath the life-rejecting emotions. The death wishes are accompanied by life wishes, which are based upon love.

But love too can be either a life-affirming or a life-sacrificing emotion. The amount of self-sacrifice in deeply suicidal persons, while seldom noted, is very great. It is the basis for the most frequent reasons given for suicide: "I am a burden," or "I hurt everyone I love," or "I am making everybody sick," and similar statements. Implicit in these reasons is the belief, "I must kill myself because I love you too much to make you suffer."

Love between spouses may be present and become deeper and more genuine in the elderly than in the young, but its strength may be unrecognized because it is more spiritual and less sensual. George Jean Nathan (1942) likened beauty to "a love that has outlasted the middle-years of life, and has met triumphantly the test of time, and faith, and cynic meditation" (p. 727). However, when love has triumphantly met the test of time, the death of the partner can be that much more unbearable. One survivor after another has described the experience of the death of a spouse as literally losing a part of the self.

The Suicidal Communication System

This section is relatively lengthy because communication is involved in all the events that culminate in a suicidal state or act. The principles of suicidogenic communication and how to transform them into life-affirming communications apply to suicidal persons at all ages. With the suicidal elderly, however, the problems are compounded because the public is bombarded with biased and pro-elderly-suicide communications by the news media. Examples include the huge free publicity given by the press to Dr. Jack Kervokian and his do-it-yourself (with a little assist from the doctor) suicide machine.

I conducted an informal poll of opinions voiced by newscasters and columnists about the suicide of 53-year-old Janet Adkins, using Dr. Kervokian's machine. The great majority criticized or condemned his action, but for a reason which illuminates the subtle anti-elderly bias that surrounds us. These commentators criticized Kervokian, not for taking a life, but because Mrs. Atkins was not old enough. Were she elderly and suffering from Alzheimer's disease, her assisted suicide would have been approved.

We are surrounded by pro-suicide-for-the-elderly propaganda, which we take in with our eyes and ears from the airwaves. Most of the elderly are not influenced to the point of seriously considering suicide. Nevertheless, there are thousands of depressed, ill, and vulnerable old people who could be influenced, especially when such life-rejecting attitudes are present within themselves and in their more intimate family systems and social circles. The media views are then confirmatory.

Communication in suicide is involved at all levels, from the socio-cultural to the individual, to most of the danger signs listed in the demographic, recognition, and family tables. The key to understanding and preventing suicide lies in the communication process.

Most studies of communication and suicide deal with only one variable, the communication of suicidal intent by the suicidal person. That is certainly important, but most such studies omit the context. They rarely describe how the communications are received or what communications preceded the expression of intent. The investigators did not look at the phenomenon from a systemic point of view or at its two-edged quality. The communication of suicidal intent can be the beginning of the end, but also the beginning of healing.

The systems concept calls attention to the transactional nature of the communication, as described by Watzlawick, Beavin, and Jackson (1967). The communication system is also mediated by family rules governing communication. These may conflict with outside rules or values such as cultural mourning customs following a loss.

Despite the power of external social mores, internal family rules are very tenacious. When the social and the family rules conflict, the outside world might be responded to as a threat to the family communication system. The therapist in such a situation may also be regarded as a threat. Family members may consequently be trapped between conflicting communication patterns:

> Rose S., at age 65, worked as a secretary at a psychiatric clinic. She was also the mother of a depressed and suicidal 40-year-old daughter. On the job Rose learned the value of direct and open communication, and in the effort to apply these principles, she asked her daughter to say what was bothering her. Her daughter did, and mother became furious. The resulting quarrel escalated and became out of control, culminating when Mrs. S. brought her daughter to the emergency room, where she was hospitalized because of an acute suicidal state.

Mrs. S. and her family were, in fact, well-meaning and well-motivated for psychotherapy. The crisis precipitated by the effort at dialogue was actually the impetus for obtaining treatment and help.

Communication is a very comprehensive term that includes all verbal and nonverbal transactions. It is impossible not to communicate; even a non-response is a communication. However, the message is not always clear and the meanings of seemingly identical communications may be different, depending upon the senders and the receivers.

As used in this presentation, communication refers to all the messages in the family that contribute specifically to the development of a suicidal act or its presentation. These include messages from a suicidal person to others and from others to a suicidal person. What is said and what is not said, who is spoken to and who is not spoken to, how the messages are sent and how they are received, are all part of the communication system.

The messages may be direct or allusive, verbal or nonverbal. "I wish I was dead," "I wish you were dead," "I wish we were dead" (this last said in preparation for suicide pacts and clusters) are all examples of life-rejecting statements. Communications also include messages that further growth and cohesion and are life saving. "I want you to live," "We can work these problems out together," "Help is available" are messages that affirm life.

The suicidal communication system is often involved in the triangling described by Brown (1978), where two persons are talking about a third who is not present, who in turn becomes the recipient of complaints or resentments for reasons which appear incomprehensible.

Communication is involved in the denial or refusal to talk about difficult or disturbing events, especially involving separation and loss. That, too, is part of the family communication system. For example, the elderly suicidal person who talks about a deceased family member is breaking a family rule of communication. The result is resentment, with the covert communication of anger and of being a burden to others. That is particularly true if there are secrets involving the deceased:

> When Rachel K.'s husband died, she expressed her grief but was not prepared for her daughter's reaction. Her daughter became agitated, distraught, and told her she did not want to hear about the death. Mrs. K. felt that she had not only lost her husband but her daughter.
>
> Mrs. K. had never been told that her husband had sexually abused their daughter throughout her teens. The daughter had married early to escape her home, divorced early, and never had a satisfying sexual relationship. She also never felt that she could speak openly about these dark and secret events. Mrs. K. felt she was a burden and made a serious suicide attempt.

Suicidogenic communications have a history of discourse that is indirect, covert, triangled, and with a minimum of open and direct dialogue. Nevertheless, the communication system is less disturbed in terms of a formal thought disorder than the systems present in the families of schizophrenic patients.

With older people the withholding of information is part of a general exclusion of the older person. An example was given in Philip Roth's memoir, *Patrimony* (1991). The author underwent an emergency quintuple by-pass operation and concealed the fact from his father, who was in his late eighties and very ill. He eventually told his father, who became very upset. "'I should have been there,' he told me in a breaking voice, the words barely words now because of what the paralysis had made of his mouth. 'I should have been there!' he repeated, this time with fury. He meant by my side at the hospital."

Alienation is accomplished, silently and insidiously, while affirmation is accomplished openly and directly. What follows are 12 typical forms of suicidal communications, with their counterparts expressing a life-affirming statement.

In all 12 of these suicidal communication patterns there is a relationship to the mechanisms of denial and projection. They perform the function of covering up a variety of events, such as the existence of suicidal behavior in the past or present in various family members, as well as a family history of sexual and aggressive acting out, including incest, murders, and other misdeeds. The fear of exposure is often behind help rejection, the avoidance of help, or the failure to utilize such help therapeutically. The indirect communications and exclusion of the person at risk result in a breakdown of cohesion and a sense of alienation.

Paradoxically, secretiveness is often combined with the need to communicate and confess. The person who becomes suicidal is frequently the one who is most open, as though it is the messenger who must die. More often, the suicidal person is an integral part of the secrecy pattern. Concealment and confession may also be combined into what may be called the suicidal conspiracy. One or more persons are told of the person's suicidal intent, and then sworn to secrecy.

The bulk of these communication patterns are not under the conscious control of the people involved, which is one reason that direct efforts to change the patterns do not work. The goal is to encourage an open, life-confirming communication system, but it is first necessary to understand and accept the communication of the family without becoming enmeshed.

The goal of treatment is for the family and patient to interact in order to form a more therapeutic communication system which can foster growth, cohesion, and autonomy. A rule of communication, therefore, is to affirm and permit the expression of grief or other unpleasant feelings directly. That may take time, but it must be realized that feelings cannot be denied, even when a crisis is necessary for their expression.

Table 5.2
Life and Death Communications

---

1. Verbalization of self-destructive wishes by the suicidal person to others,
    versus
    Verbalization of wishes to live, often expressed as problem-resolution wishes.

2. Verbal or nonverbal communications by significant others that the suicidal person commit suicide,
    versus
    Communications that the suicidal other is valued, important, appreciated, and needed, with wishes that the other live.

3. Communications of anger, depression, and despair by significant others at expressions of autonomy by the potentially suicidal person,
    versus
    Expressions by significant others of pleasure in achievement, competence, autonomy, and other manifestations of adaptation and functioning by the person.

4. Nonverbal body and facial expressions of anger, despair, and fear,
    versus
    Nonverbal expressions of confidence and support.

5. The suicidal act as the message,
    versus
    Life-affirming acts as the message, such as hugging, bringing a gift, going out together.

6. Illness "caused" by the potential suicide,
    versus
    Improved function "caused" by the person at risk, such as asking the person for help in dealing with a problem.

7. A turning away movement,
    versus
    Turning toward.

8. Leaving, especially at the height of an argument,
    versus
    Staying with the person.

9. Imperviousness or non-receptivity of suicidal message,
    versus
    Responding directly in a caring manner.

10. Failure to notify others,
    versus
    Telling others.

11. Covert and indirect communications,
    versus
    Open and direct dialogue.

12. Secretiveness,
    versus
    Sharing of communications.

An Intolerance for Crises

A crisis is a call for change. However, as Pittman (1987) pointed out, a crisis can also be utilized to prevent change, and in the family vulnerable to suicide, to prevent separation. The crisis often communicates the presence of an untenable and intolerable situation with no way out. At least that is how it is perceived. The task is to change the perception.

The older the person the greater the number of crises of loss and separation, of role changes, isolation, illness, and decline, each one of which may take its toll. The accumulation of such crises helps make the already vulnerable elderly person still more vulnerable to a suicidal state.

The family is intimately involved with these experiences. Separation, loss, and bereavement become combined with perceived threats to the family system, while role changes and the vicissitudes of changing interpersonal relationships in one elderly person necessitate changes in all the family members. At the time of a suicidal state all of these family characteristics escalate into one massive and dangerous crisis. Nevertheless, these crises represent an opportunity as well as a danger. That is why all treatment of the suicidal begins with a comprehensive assessment and crisis intervention, preferably family crisis intervention.

FAMILY THERAPY

The general principles of family treatment at all ages have been presented in my previous writings (Richman, 1986). The value of my family approach has been particularly recognized for suicidal adolescents and young adults (Kaplan & Maldaver, 1990). This book is a response to the compelling need to apply the family-oriented approach to an evaluation and treatment of suicidal states in late life. In the process, new information and experiences are presented.

At all ages the family of the suicidal person is both a source of stress and conflict and of healing and cure. Family therapy taps into their hidden powers, resources, and wellsprings of love.

Double Bonds and Double Binds

Families are held together by ties that are extremely strong but not always evident to the seemingly objective observer. Boszermenyi-Nagy and Spark (1973) called these ties "invisible loyalties." They are based upon obligations, demands, family legends, rules, and myths that are rarely made explicit, but possess great strength. They can be considered the unconscious of the family system.

Get the family together in the sheltered situation of an accepting therapist, and that unconscious can be made conscious in a constructive and cohesive manner. That can occur because these loyalties are based upon a special kind of caring; and again, as happens so frequently, they are best understood by artists and story tellers.

Swados probably understood the troubled children in *Runaways* so well because of her own painful experiences with mentally ill members of her family. However, these invisible loyalties are universal. They do not belong only in the province of those who are troubled or disturbed. That is why Wiesel's description of "The Rothschilds" strikes such a universal chord.

Family therapy respects these loyalties. However, the treatment may be complicated by the fears and resistance of the family and patient, and their uncertainty regarding whether to reject or accept the therapist. The double bind is symbolically represented humorously by Joseph Heller in his novel *Good As Gold* (1979). The hero, Bruce Gold, meets his new stepmother and she says to him, "I would like to think of you all as my very own children. Please call me mother." Gold replied, "Very well, Mother. Welcome to the family." "I'm not your mother," she snapped.

Mr. Heller had the artist's ability to understand double bind situations, where whatever the therapist does is "wrong" or "bad," and the therapist feels trapped and enmeshed. As one of my more ambivalent patients remarked, "If you don't see me, I will kill myself, and if you see me, I will kill myself" (reported in Richman, 1986). I did continue to see her and she did not kill herself.

My work relies upon the understanding that the family as a system is based upon the positive affective components of loyalty and devotion, love and caring, extending through time and generations and through space, wherever the family members are.

Conflicted Loyalties

The confusion and ambivalence of the suicidal state in the elderly may be related to the re-arousal of conflicts from the past combined with role failures in the present. The nature of this unfinished business in the family was discussed earlier in this chapter. Especially in a family where old resentment and unresolved conflicts are rife, role loss and failure can be the last straw.

The persistence of the past means that a serious illness in the potentially suicidal old person may be reacted to by an upsurge of rage in the family members over past misdeeds or neglect, and this may precipitate a suicidal state. The rage and other disruptive reactions emphasize the importance of bringing in the family. However, such a step may be problematic when the family members cling to their old hurts and are resistant.

The most therapeutic response to resistance is to maintain a positive, family-oriented approach. The positive potentials of such a resurfacing of old resentments should not be overlooked. They offer family members an opportunity for a second chance later in life to contact the painful conflicts of their youth, resolve them, and to overcome roadblocks and continue growth in the entire family:

> Nicholas F. cut his wrists savagely while in a nursing home where he had been recently placed following a stroke. He also deflected his anger onto the staff of the home where he lived. His daughter refused to see him or participate in therapy, because, she said, he had mistreated his wife, her mother, and neglected her when she was a child. Thus he became the center of discord in every area of his interpersonal life. However, both his wife and his daughter were willing to talk to the therapist over the phone.
>
> During therapy sessions, he established a more positive relationship with the nursing home, and, as he put it, "picked up the pieces." The sessions included letter writing to other relatives from whom he had been estranged. As a result he renewed his relationship with his surviving sister.

You can reach a family that refuses to come in a variety of ways: by working with the individual, using the phone, bringing in other relatives, and above all by remaining empathic and understanding of all participants. Family therapy may be symbolized by the slogan, "one family indivisible, with empathy and understanding for all."

Both group and family therapy are valuable for restoring a sense of worth, because the self-esteem and sense of self of the suicidal are so dependent upon how they are regarded. The family meetings most often confirm that they are wanted, or at least not completely rejected, and have a place. That is true, especially when the old unresolved anger must first be aired. Group therapy, as we shall see, is particularly valuable for role restoration.

Love and loyalty may also conflict with other forces based upon past resentments, yet the positive feelings may win out:

> George S.'s wife was still filled with resentment at his desertion of her and their children 25 years ago. He ran off with her best friend, whose life and

marriage were also ruined. After he made a suicide attempt, he became my patient. I took steps to arrange a family meeting, and spoke to his ex-wife on the phone. She was eager to pour out her story. I listened and was certainly sympathetic, understanding, and empathic. It was clear that he had been a destructive, selfish bastard. I said that I was his therapist and committed to helping him.

She fully understood, and said she would cooperate, and so she did. Mr. S. was seen in family therapy with his three children, which was instrumental in carrying the treatment to a successful conclusion. The success, I believe, was due to his ex-wife giving the children permission to participate in the therapy, even though she herself refused to attend. (However, she did insist upon hearing about the sessions, in detail.)

Mrs. S.'s cooperation was based upon the forces of loyalty and love which remained dormant but never died, and therefore defeated anger and hate. During the family meetings, the old conflicts were confronted and aired. His children reproached their father for deserting them and his wife. The encounter began a movement towards reconciliation. Therapy was terminated when the patient moved to a residence closer to his family.

As a general rule, therapy with the older suicidal person involves this arousal and resolution of old unfinished business. The Oedipal nature of these early conflicts is noteworthy. The endurance of generation conflicts, continuing when the "children" are middle-aged and the parents elderly, has become more prevalent in this age of increasing longevity (Wolinsky, 1990).

Sometimes the task of the family is to achieve a greater closeness, and sometimes a greater distance, as in the following situation of Dorothy D. and her daughter:

Dorothy D. was a 68-year-old widow who lived with one of her daughters. The daughter had never come to terms with her feelings of early maternal deprivation. When the daughter invited her mother to move in with her, she proceeded to repeat the pattern of felt rejection and neglect, but with the mother–daughter roles reversed. This time, the mother was neglected, but ordered in Cinderella fashion to shop, clean, cook, and take care of the children. The mother regularly became suicidal, with no apparent reason or precipitant, and would be hospitalized.

During her most recent hospitalization the therapist assigned to Mrs. D. met regularly with the daughter to help her accept the placement of her mother in a nearby adult residence. The daughter was very resistant, but finally acceded, saying in a little child's voice, "I'll have to accept that I never had a real Mommy."

Mrs. D. and her daughter were stuck in a rigid, repetitive early pattern. The suicidal behavior had a positive message: this old pattern no longer worked. Mrs. D. moved to the adult home near her daughter. Their relationship immediately improved. She also established an active social life of her own in the home. Her daughter, meanwhile, advanced in her profession, where she had been stuck previously.

Unresolved early conflicts and the persistence of past resentments helped explain the endurance of the suicidal state in Dorothy D. as in many elderly patients.

The Dangers of Side Taking

The destructive interactions can be best understood as a projection upon the potentially suicidal person of the vulnerability of the partner and other family members. At the same time that they are blaming the suicidal person for all the ills in the family, they are exquisitely sensitive to any hint of personal blame or responsibility. Many a treatment has been terminated when the therapist sided with the patient or criticized the family.

There is a strong quality of unbearable but buried guilt in these families. The suicidal person is driven not only by his or her own guilty conscience or superego, but represents the harsh superego of the entire family in the form of shame, guilt, remorse, and finally atonement through the suicidal act.

That is why positive humor, properly utilized, can be therapeutic, because it puts the person in contact with the more loving and forgiving superego. The family that can laugh together cannot have a suicidal member. But even in the most loving of families, clearing up misunderstandings is a life-long task which can continue even until the last moments of existence.

The intrinsic caring and growth forces can be considered the wisdom of the family as well as the individual. Perhaps not every family possesses that wisdom, although I believe they possess at least the potential. It is tapped into by listening to the family, considering their wishes and recommendations, and realizing they may have the key to overcoming the suicidal state in their midst, no matter how much they conflict with the therapist's orientation.

I do not try to change the family pattern. The family system and its roots in cultural and ethnic traditions are accepted and respected. Therapeutic contact with the family results in decreased separation anxiety and increased individuation and competence in the suicidal patient and others.

A Family Interview For Beginning All Therapy

The treatment of the suicidal individual is not independent of the relationship between other family members with the therapist. That means establishing contact with all of the family members, sometimes including those who do not attend. The wife of George S., for example, told her children she would not attend the meetings because she did not want me to see that she was an unattractive old lady.

There is a transference that takes place within the family in those who have never seen the therapist, as well as a countertransference of the therapist with those unseen (but not necessarily unheard). Sometimes the transference takes the form of a preconceived negative attitude towards psychotherapy or any other form of psychiatric-related intervention. Sometimes there is a projection of self-esteem problems, with a belief that the therapist will be critical and rejecting.

This complex pattern of transference and countertransference reactions and expectations makes one procedure essential: It is important that the therapist see the family at the beginning of treatment, even if the therapy is not to be family-oriented. With members who refused to attend, it may be helpful to initiate some telephone contact:

Jerome R., age 78, and Nora R., age 75, were referred by Mr. R.'s internist, specifically for couple's therapy. Mr. R. had asthma, emphysema, cardiac illness, and a host of other ailments, all of which were exacerbated by severe conflicts with his wife. The marital conflicts escalated to dangerous levels once the last of their four children left the home.

The couple seemed to respond well to therapy, both of them ventilated their complaints, fought with the other, and competed for the therapist's approval. Mr. R.'s physical condition quickly improved. However, they regularly stopped coming after three or four sessions, returned at the insistence of their internist, but stopped again.

They were very resistant to a family session; but a meeting was finally arranged with difficulty, because their children all lived out of town. The three daughters were particularly concerned about their parents' quarrels and the life-threatening consequences. They were pleased at the therapist's understanding of the situation, his concentration upon the here-and-now and of the need to reduce marital tensions.

At the end of the session the eldest daughter said that she had misunderstood what was involved in therapy. She thought it consisted of going back to the past and forcing her parents to bring out every conflict and resentment between them. She sees, however, that it was not like that. Mr. and Mrs. R. had interpreted their daughter's negative attitude as a message for them to reject therapy.

This one family therapy session marked a turning point in the treatment, with a permanent change from covert resistance to working therapeutic alliance.

Each therapist has his or her personal style and preferred procedures. Reframing, relabeling, paradoxical interventions and a search for what has worked well for the family members in the past are among the fruitful therapeutic procedures. Minuchin (1974), for example, saw a mother and son in an intense symbiotic relationship. He prescribed exaggerated symbiotic behavior, which included their being together a hundred percent of the time, even to the point of sleeping together. When he gave them permission to separate, they were relieved and grateful.

When I gave that example during a talk in Brooklyn, five people in the audience came over separately to tell me the Yiddish story of a woman who came to a Rabbi complaining that their house was unbearably small and overcrowded. He instructed the woman to place all of the farm animals into the house in addition to all of the people. Gradually, he allowed her to remove the animals one by one. She thanked him because the house was now so roomy.

Acceptance of the Family Lifestyle

Intervening, especially to "change" a symptom or family pattern before knowing its function and perhaps its survival value is always undesirable. The example of the teacher in the movie "Dead Poets Society" is a valid one. He was a charismatic individual who encouraged a pupil to become an actor, despite the opposition of his parents. The resulting conflict precipitated the suicide of the student.

A less tragic example of an unsuccessful effort to enforce change was reported by Horewitz (1979) in his treatment of a couple who used up all their energies in fighting with each other. They participated calmly in the therapy sessions until just before the end of the session. "Then all hell broke loose." The therapist finally arranged to intervene in their "uproar-on-leaving pattern." For the nest session, "Lillie and John began their verbal battle just as their usual hour was ending." The therapist then announced that they had an extra hour available to see the problem through. At the end of that hour all the participants were worn out, but the couple had resolved their angry fighting. There was only one problem: they never came back. "And I never heard from either of them again" (p. 228).

Once again the lesson is that conflicts are overcome not by intruding or controlling but by working with the family. The family pattern must be accepted no matter how maladaptive it may seem. No interventions can be made without empathy and a clear understanding of the function performed by the behavior or family pattern.

A major task of the therapist is to accept and then deal with the turmoil of feelings inculcated by the rage, depression, and pain of the suicidal person and family. First, the expression of these extreme and negative feelings is encouraged. Second, they are relabeled (validly) as the result of frustration and helplessness. These interventions are part of the task of reducing separation anxiety and other stresses behind the family discord.

Acceptance of the family means accepting the worth and existence of each individual member. In the family this need for affirmation of the individual can sometimes be forgotten, neglected, or perceived as a threat. Where suicide is a problem, no matter what the age, each and every member of the family is to be regarded as in extreme need of individual attention. The nonthreatening affirmation of the self can take place most effectively in the family setting, often combined with individual sessions:

> In family sessions, Mrs. T., whose daughter had died suddenly, was helped to grieve and to accept this tragic loss. She expressed much appreciation for the support she had received and a degree of family closeness that was greater than ever before.
>
> In individual sessions, the patient revealed how upset and alone she continued to feel. She felt relieved after crying and airing her grief. However, upon entering her lonely apartment, she would become overwhelmed once again with the sense of loss of her daughter.
>
> Recently she has reported changing perceptions in a positive direction of her life experiences and their meaning. For example, she recalled the loving experiences she observed between her late daughter and her daughter's husband and children. Between sobs she declared how happy she was for the good life her daughter had had. She also displayed the fortunate facility to use denial adaptively. For example, she was able to downplay her daughter's drinking and recall their pleasurable conversations.
>
> Nevertheless, she found the individual sessions distressing and the family meetings enjoyable. Both were necessary, leading to a more holistic integration.
>
> In family sessions her surviving daughter and son-in-law have insisted upon speaking in detail about the difficulties and disturbed behavior exhibited by the deceased daughter. These had been concealed from the patient for

years, on the grounds that it would upset her too much. I listened to this material feeling the pain that the patient felt, especially since denial had been a major part of her lifestyle throughout her 80 years. "Would you rather not hear this?" I asked. "Of course not," she replied. "I want to know the truth."

The family, in its wisdom, knew how much she could tolerate and were in touch with her strengths, perhaps more than I was. This example also illustrates a value of longer term therapy with suicidal people. The patient could not have dealt with such charged material as constructively as she did were she only in brief therapy. Her suicidal urge was reduced significantly very early in therapy and treatment could have been discontinued, but continued therapy made her life richer.

The Family as the Client

Suicidal behavior in the elderly can often be traced to a family system under threat or stress, often with the belief that its survival is threatened. The problem is attributed to the suicidal person, thus allowing the family or partner to avoid dealing with what is really going on in order to maintain an untenable relationship.

A similar pattern was reported by Canetto, Feldman, and Lupei (1989) in a study of hospitalized suicidal patients and their partners. The suicidal person was regularly presented as the problem. However, the difficulties involving the nonsuicidal partners were mutual and transactional, with "a propensity toward anaclitic, need-satisfying attitudes and relationships" (p. 203).

Analogous findings were reported many years ago by Tabachnick (1961) in his studies of couples where one person was suicidal but both were involved in disturbed symbiotic relationships.

The reaction to separation and loss, especially through death, is not an individual matter. The loss of a spouse or other loved one often precipitates a suicidal act when other family members cannot deal with the situation, especially when mourning is forbidden.

The relatives and other significant persons perceive the mourning of the one who becomes suicidal as damaging to the others. Family therapy is recommended, not only because the family is the source of healing but because the suicidal act communicates the presence of an entire family in trouble and in need of help:

The grandchildren of Mrs. T. disclosed that their mother had been a closet alcoholic who died as the result of a fall. This was information they felt they had to conceal from their grandmother. Consequently the grandmother's appropriate expression of grief aroused great conflict in the grandchildren. In therapy, as we have seen, other members of the family continued opening up the family system by airing information about the deceased daughter and also about themselves. The grandchildren were also able to express their depression and anger at their deceased mother.

The above example illustrates both the degree to which disturbed communication enters into the suicidal state, and the dynamic reasons why the family believes direct communication is dangerous. Mrs. T. was responding more appropriately to the loss of her daughter than anyone else in her family, but in effect, she was banished for the crime of mourning.

As we have seen, suicidal communication includes the denial or refusal to talk about difficult or disturbing events, especially those involving separation and loss. The suicidal person who talks about a deceased family member, as did Mrs. T. and so many other bereaved men and women, was breaking that family rule of communication. The result is resentment and the covert communication of anger and of being a burden to others.

The Treatment of Suicide Pacts

Suicide pact ideation occurs more frequently among elderly couples than is commonly realized. Such ideation can be understood and responded to as valuable communications, leading to major steps towards recovery from the suicidal state:

> Theodore and Frances C. entered therapy after Mr. C. became depressed and suicidal, and was referred to the psycho-geriatric clinic by his physician. He was 78; she, 15 years younger. His depression followed a medical diagnosis of cancer, and his suicidal preoccupations continued although his condition was being treated successfully.
>
> The more immediate precipitant was the departure of their youngest daughter from the home, to live with a boyfriend. Mr. C. was seen in individual therapy and for medication with one therapist, and the couple was seen in marital and family therapy by another. They were treated successfully, and upon termination both were no longer depressed and suicidal.
>
> Mr. C. reported that "they" were contemplating suicide. Mrs. C. nodded in agreement. They were surprised when asked why she needed to commit suicide if he did. He explained that they were so much one person that she could not survive alone. They were surprised again when asked how their children would deal with the loss of both parents simultaneously. "I never thought of that," said Mrs. C.

Other couples were less fortunate. As we have seen, popular maga-
zines and other news media contain many articles about suicide pacts. A
general attitude of approval pervades these narratives. Many of these
suicides were preventable, the couples were treatable, and they could
have been helped towards a greater closeness and richness of existence
for the time remaining to them. However, few media reports criticize or
disapprove of the suicide pact, or even state that there are workable alternatives.

Rather than a rational act by people who do not choose to live alone
without the other, suicide pacts communicate a problem in the couple
and family system that needs resolution. The couple feels trapped, and
they have either rejected help, do not know how to obtain the needed
help, or have received the wrong kind of help. I hope that the slanted
pro-suicide accounts in the media of pacts in the elderly do not keep
people with suicide pact ideation from obtaining the therapy which can
be effective and life saving.

Similar reflections apply to murder-suicides, or even to so-called
"mercy killings":

> One of the most celebrated cases involved Rosswell Gilbert, who lived with
> his wife in a retirement community in Florida. She developed Alzheimer's
> disease; he could not cope with her illness and finally shot her to death. He
> was found guilty of murder by the Florida courts and sentenced to 25 years in
> jail.

Many of the social problems in Florida involving suicide are handled by
the legal system. The Rosswell Gilbert case is a typical example. When
he shot his wife he not only committed an illegal act; he called attention
to a major social problem that needed resolution. That problem was the
effect upon the family and other loved ones of Alzheimer's disease and
other chronic ailments. Support groups and family therapy could help
relatives and make such drastic and tragic behavior necessary. That
would be far preferable to punishment. Instead, Florida "punished the
guilty" and consequently nothing needed to change and no social measures were instituted.

> A similar example but with a different outcome involved Arnold M., a
> 78-year-old man, who was referred to me after he spoke to the neurologist
> who confirmed that his wife had an advanced case of Alzheimer's disease. In
> addition, their only son, age 40, was retarded and brain damaged, and unable
> to function without the care of his parents, or so it was believed. Mr. M. con-
> fided to the doctor that he planned to kill his wife and son and then himself.

I saw him immediately in individual and family therapy, with a crisis-oriented approach. He and his wife also joined a group for Alzheimer's patients and their relatives. In the group Mr. M. was able to ventilate his murder–suicide thoughts with complete understanding from the other group members, which was of great help in resolving his crisis.

In the family sessions their son proved to be a remarkably sensitive and perceptive person, who was very concerned about his parents. In his own way he was mature and competent. He volunteered for many activities and belonged to a social group for the retarded. There, he had recently met a woman about his age, and they had established a close, intimate relationship. Mr. M. reacted with rage and refused to let the girlfriend into the house, on the grounds that she was fat and that she smelled. But it was then that he decided that it was necessary to kill his wife, his son, and himself. It was not that his son needed his mother and father and could not function on his own, but rather that he was becoming increasingly independent and self sufficient. He no longer needed his father, which posed an unbearable threat to his self-esteem, as well as one other anticipated loss.

This case contrasts dramatically with that of Rosswell Gilbert in Florida. There are other people who have been helped through support groups and a comprehensive approach. Society needs more such help, not more punishment.

A strong symbiotic relationship among elderly couples is not only very frequent, but has many positive potentials. Symbiosis can become the basis for productive and creative activities and relationships, rather than the foundation of hopelessness and despair. One task in therapy with the suicidal elderly is to transform the destructive interactions into positive aspects of symbiosis. In a well-functioning family or couple, relationships are neither entirely autonomous, as in those who are isolated, or completely undifferentiated, as in those whose ties have meant the loss of their individual selves. Instead, there is an optimal relationship between individual development and permeable boundaries.

Such flexibility is a prerequisite for maturity. For example, creative activity and playful regression in the service of the ego is characteristic of the artistic and creative person. Such regression, as described by Kris (1952), requires the ego strength and the capacity to lose boundaries and merge, either playfully or in love, and then re-emerge with one's individuality intact.

To sum up, the family-oriented treatment of suicidal people begins with family-crisis intervention. The immediate goal after physical life-saving measures is that of reducing separation and death anxiety and the often overwhelming feeling by the family of being burdened. Decreasing these anxieties and tensions reduces the immediate risk of suicide while facilitating a more enduring long-term growth and development of all the family members. Therapy moves from a suicidal crisis and a seemingly inexorable destructive family process, to a family health process which affirms both the autonomy of each member and the cohesiveness of the family structure. Through the release of the positive resources of the family, a life-affirming family therapy approach saves lives in the future.

Family therapy is the most challenging but also the most rewarding treatment for the suicidal elderly. All successful therapy with suicidal people is family therapy in the sense that family relations and interactions become constructive, cohesive, accepting of autonomy, and non-destructive.

Therapy with married elderly couples contains the promise of achieving a degree of closeness and intimacy which was less available when work and other activities were used for avoidance. Group therapy, which is described in the following chapter, or couples group therapy, which combines the benefit of marital and group treatment, facilitate an adaptive intimacy.

With some couples, however, the problem is that of too much closeness, so that individual growth is hampered. Marital and couples group therapy is still recommended, combined with individual therapy. When the suicidal person is not married but single, divorced, or widowed, then the problem is often that of loneliness and isolation. The recommendation is once again for group and family therapy, often combined with individual sessions. All these reflections emphasize the value of a flexible, multi-determined approach.

6

Group Psychotherapy with Suicidal Patients

Group therapy is intrinsically suited for elderly suicidal persons because of the prevalence of social isolation, losses, the decline in competence and abilities, the roles lost, and especially the loss of spouses, friends, and other significant persons. All of these culminate in an overwhelming sense of alienation, rejection, and worthlessness.

Durkheim's statement that suicide is related to the loss of social integration is a statistic based upon the accumulated sufferings of millions of people. In human terms, the greater the alienation, the greater the risk; the greater the integration, the less the risk. Group psychotherapy helps restore social cohesion through the procedures described in this chapter.

In the group, a person who feels crushed by adversity, worthless, and without skills finds that what he or she says is listened to and respected. There is a restoration of roles instead of the loss and breakdown of earlier roles that had so damaged his or her self-esteem. Such role restoration and role maintenance can occur through the affirmation of the group and its stimulation of the knowledge, wisdom, understanding, and other assets of the depressed and suicidal older person. However, it must be understood that many elderly people may be resistant to group therapy for personal reasons and would benefit by initially beginning with a one-on-one therapist relationship before progressing to group therapy (See Chapter 7).

A HISTORICAL NOTE

Group psychotherapy has found an accepted and even honored place in the treatment of suicidal patients, but such was not always the case. The early history of group psychotherapy is dominated more by the exclusion of suicidal patients than their acceptance. Several reports of group therapy members who committed suicide gave therapists the message to preclude patients with such problems.

As early as 1951 Bachrach recommended that suicidal patients be excluded from group psychotherapy (Bachrach, 1951). Bowers, Mullan, and Berkowitz (1959) emphasized the ever-present possibility of suicide in a therapy group, and its potentially traumatic effect on other group members. Similarly, McCourtney (1961) speculated that the group process "may activate the death wish and encourage the group member to commit suicide" (p. 897). Responding to such reports, Strickler and Allgeyer (1967), in a pioneering work on crisis-oriented group therapy, specifically excluded patients who were suicidal. Written at a time when the special value of homogeneous groups was not recognized, they were probably right.

Positive group therapy experiences with suicidal members were also reported. Miller and Shaskan (1963) presented a case of a suicidal man who was treated successfully in a heterogeneous group with psychotic and sociopathic members. The authors attributed his improvement to "the permissive nature of the group." Evidently, the group fostered a sense of belonging, acceptance, and cohesiveness. However, as we have seen, most other reports had been much less sanguine. The general consensus was to be very cautious about accepting a suicidal person into group psychotherapy.

Nevertheless, such attitudes began to change, influenced by some pioneers who began to experiment, usually under the sheltering wings of a hospital ward or suicide-prevention center. In 1966, Indin started a group with eight women, all suicidal, in a closed psychiatric ward. The results were encouraging, although Indin had to deal with the anxiety and resistance of other staff members (Indin, 1966).

About the same time, Reiss (1968) observed similar positive dynamics and results in an informal group of six individuals on a psychiatric ward, all with a history of suicidal behavior. The patients in this group, which had formed spontaneously, had previously tended to form self-destructive dyads, in which each would instigate the other into committing suicidal acts. After the "suicide six" formed their own group, which was somewhat like a clique, none committed any further suicidal acts. However, the group dissolved after the hospital staff finally intervened, unable to tolerate a group organized and run by patients without control by staff members.

Major theoretical as well as practical implications arise from the Reiss and Indin articles. There is a life-affirming power in groups of people who have problems in common, i.e., homogeneous groups. When *two* suicidal people get together, they stimulate each other's self-destructive behavior. An example reported by Berman (1990) concerned two women, "patients A and C," in their mid-thirties, who were being seen by two different therapists. They met when both were hospitalized following suicide attempts. They instigated each other into suicidal acts and other behaviors which represented an acting out against the therapists. Both eventually killed themselves.

The deadly dyad, as illustrated by Berman and many others, is based upon a transference or repetition outside the family of a dysfunctional pattern inside the family. In this pattern, two people, often representing a mother and child, are in alliance against a third person, such as the father.

The suicidal behavior emerges when one member of a dyad has to differentiate into a more autonomous self under the pressure of developmental demands or life circumstances. The destructive acting out can then represent a negative transference against the therapist, the hospital system, or some other parent-figure.

TOWARD SUICIDE-PREVENTION GROUPS

One solution is to change the situation from a dyad to a group setting. Such a move changes the rules and meanings of the behavior. Two suicidal people together instigate each other to self-destructive behavior. A gathering of three or more suicidal people, however, arouses caring, rescuing and life-enhancing forces. These positive effects may be due to dynamics similar to those found in other homogeneous groups such as the bereaved, paraplegics, cancer patients, and other ill or disabled persons.

The value of these homogeneous groups of suicidal persons has been increasingly recognized. Ross and Motto (1984) described such groups for suicidal adolescents, while Billings et al. (1974), Comstock and McDermott (1975), Farberow (1968, 1972), and Hackel and Asimos (1981) have written on non-geriatric adults. The success of these efforts has stimulated the formation of additional groups throughout the country.

Nevertheless, one major group was excluded: the suicidal elderly. For example, the comprehensive book on group psychotherapies for the elderly, edited by MacLennan, Saul, and Weiner (1988), contained no references to the suicidal aside from a brief discussion by Tross and Blum (1988) of the wish to die. Similarly, the thorough review and annotated bibliography by Osgood and McIntosh (1986) on suicide in the elderly contained no references to group psychotherapy. That was no oversight; there are no such references.

I therefore organized a group for depressed and suicidal geriatric patients. This chapter describes what group therapy can contribute, how and why it works, its major goals, the patients who benefit the most, the major themes and procedures, and the typical experiences that take place, especially as illustrated in one extensive case narration.

Much resistance to homogeneous group therapy programs has taken place, because they introduce a new procedure into a stable existing system (Hackel & Asimos, 1981). Some settings have welcomed innovative approaches. Fortunately, my group for depressed and suicidal geriatric patients was one of these.

Setting and Subjects

The group members were all patients at the outpatient psychogeriatric clinic attached to a city hospital. Referrals were obtained from medical clinics, inpatient wards, and private physicians. About ten percent were self-referred, on the basis of recommendations from friends or other professionals. The ages of the patients ranged from 68 to 84, with the average being in the mid-seventies. Depressive symptoms, retirement, illness, and becoming widowed or suffering other losses were the most frequent presenting complaints.

The qualifications for admission to the group included the presence of a major depression or suicidal behavior and symptoms. The ability to understand and communicate with others was essential. The severely hearing impaired, for example, were not admitted. On the other hand, those with dementia or other organic impairments were accepted if they were able to comprehend, attend, and respond to others.

Ninety percent of the patients in the group carried the diagnosis of an affective condition. The predominant one was "Major Depressive Disorder," either recurrent or a first episode. One or two patients at any one time were diagnosed as bipolar, and occasionally, one had a diagnosis of psychosis. The presence of manic or hypomanic group members generally had a facilitating effect, by maintaining the level of communication and occasionally injecting a lighter tone.

In addition, this was also a personality disorder group. Over two-thirds of the group members met the requirements for the diagnostic category of "Borderline," with the typical instability of emotions and relationships, and acting out. Most were on antidepressants or psychotropic medication. Most also had some medical or physical ailment, such as cardiac disease, pulmonary disorders, Parkinson's, stroke or other neurological conditions, and malignancies.

The group was predominantly white, with a small number of black and Hispanic members, but they could just as well have been more ethnically heterogeneous. I saw no differences in outcome or group interactions that could be attributed to ethnic or cultural characteristics. Suicide and depression create a democracy based upon mutual concerns.

All candidates for the group were screened carefully and interviewed by myself as well as a psychiatrist who was the clinic director. The patients were initially seen with relatives in a family interview, which is a routine part of my intake and assessment process. Urgent problems were dealt with before admission to the group. If patients were in crisis, crisis intervention was instituted. Family therapy was provided if significant areas of family tension were present or if the relatives were particularly supportive and willing to participate.

During the initial interviews the patients were told about the group and invited to attend. In addition to the group, the treatment was coordinated with other professionals and institutions which were involved, such as physicians, hospitals, and social agencies. Group therapy was but one part of a comprehensive treatment plan.

Because group therapy was virtually never the only therapy, that sometimes led to problems. Some patients would reserve their significant information and relationship for the therapist and withhold their participation in the group. That occurred, too, with those who had previously been in individual therapy. It was as though they perceived the group as conflicting with the one-to-one relationship with the therapist.

The solution was to prepare them more fully and obtain their agreement to be as open as possible and to participate in the group; otherwise they were not accepted. The rule was flexible because some patients, who were not cooperative, nevertheless needed such treatment with its opportunity for controlled interaction with others. In addition, this homogeneous group therapy for the elderly suicidal and depressed was still in an exploratory stage. We all needed to learn which patients were most suitable for the group, which ones benefit and why, and what the group experience can or cannot provide.

An Outline of the Group Therapy Process

The group members usually set the agenda and determined what to discuss, with the therapist monitoring the process and the content. The topics ranged widely, from medical and emotional complaints to family and interpersonal problems, loneliness, and the non-acceptance of aging. All of these problems are also typically expressed in other geriatric groups.

Three other themes formed a relatively unique pattern that could not have been expressed as openly in a heterogeneous group. These were: first, the sharing of experiences around hospitalization and electric shock therapy; second, the feeling of being a burden to others; and third, the presence of suicidal impulses and behavior.

I originally waited for these three topics to arise spontaneously, but found that too often members kept such thoughts from the group. I therefore began to monitor the presence of these areas without necessarily waiting for someone to mention them. At or near the beginning of the session I would ask each group member about depression, suicidal urges, difficulties coping, and feelings of being a burden. When these were expressed, spontaneously or through inquiry, I routinely asked the group to respond to what had been said. They did, displaying a skill, sensitivity, and a healing touch that extended beyond the ordinary boundaries.

At any one time, most participants said they were not seriously depressed or suicidal. Nevertheless, this was a vulnerable group, and it was best to err on the side of caution and assume that all were potentially suicidal or profoundly depressed.

There were usually one or two members who virtually always said they were suicidal. They were encouraged to state why, very specifically. There is a danger with such patients of a "cry wolf" syndrome in which others become inured and disregard the possible emergence of a more genuine and serious suicidal state. That is less likely in a homogeneous group where the members are more in touch with each other's experiences and danger signs. (An example is given later in this chapter in the case of Peter V.)

As noted, neurological impairment was not necessarily a barrier to admission into the group. In fact, patients who had been subjected to such conditions were often singularly free to deal with the associated conditions, knowing that they are among friends:

Nathan F., for example, shared the results of his CT scan with the group. The doctor explained to him, he said, that his brain was atrophying and he had had numerous small strokes. He added that he was concerned, but not depressed, quite unlike his former reactions to stress. During the group session he listened and participated actively. When the subject of suicide arose, for example, he urged the person not to despair and usually offered examples from his own difficult life. He was alert and able to mobilize his cognitive abilities, especially in the group situation.

Such experiences in the group have made me more optimistic about the unrealized possibilities present in many of those who are organically impaired, particularly when combined with specialized treatment procedures such as Sensory Training (Richman, 1969). Some organically impaired people can make contributions beyond what they accomplished earlier. An example is James Brady, who was shot in the head during the assassination attempt on President Reagan. With his help and that of his wife, the gun law, known popularly as the Brady Bill, may eventually save many lives.

GROUP THERAPY AND THE LIFE REVIEW

Therapy involving reminiscence and the life review is especially to be recommended in group work with the elderly because of the opportunities for sharing a body of experiences in common. The result is an increase in cohesion and a sense of belonging. This may be more true in age homogeneous groups because their stories may not be understood or appreciated as much by earlier generations.

Ego integrity, Erikson's last stage of development, involves looking at one's life and tying it all together into a meaningful whole. Such ego integrity is actualized in group therapy by the life review. The therapist need not actively foster the life review; it emerges naturally and spontaneously in the elderly.

The life review is an intrinsic part of group sessions. Get a group of elderly people together and they start to tell stories. They talk about their aches and pains and various ailments; they complain about their children or world conditions. Gradually, they begin to talk about their depression, say, or conflicts with family members. Others share similar experiences, offering understanding, empathy, plenty of advice, and much wisdom.

Most of all, they tell stories, and get better. The life review ties together the past and the present, and consequently the meaning of one's entire life becomes illuminated. The nature and meaning of experience has become transformed.

It was with some disappointment that I read of William Styron's (1990) dislike of group therapy during his treatment for depression. I was surprised because group therapy is a province par excellence for the storyteller. I became less surprised when he described the group leader as someone who seemed particularly inept, inexperienced, and unempathic. In the right group, William Styron could have listened to stories from his comrades in pain and shared his own stories with them, and all would have profited from the experience.

COMMUNICATION AND GROUP THERAPY

The communications of patients with similar problems and dynamics resonate with each other. Stone (1991) gave an example of a group where a new member remained silent despite several invitations by the therapist to respond. Another new member talked about the social diffi- culties he experienced because of being hospitalized and in treatment for a "mental illness." Other group members shared similar experi- ences. At this point the silent newcomer spoke up and described similar problems in her life.

Such sensitive and therapeutic contacts occur frequently in homoge- neous group therapy, where the responses of the group members dis- play an intrinsic understanding.

Norman H. declared that he is not able to deal with the stress surrounding the marriage of his son and the wedding arrangements. His wife has been having temper outbursts during which she says she hates Norman, and all their troubles are the fault of his illness. He now feels suicidal.

Bernard T., seemingly changing the subject, told of an incident when he overreacted with rage at a remark made by a friend. The relation of similar suppressed rage to Mr. H's depression and suicidal feelings quickly became apparent. Mr. H. responded that he cannot express his anger for fear of losing control.

The shared communications often involved suicidal impulses and their alleviation. The process can best be understood in the context of the person's life history, as illustrated in the story of Mr. V:

I received a call from a social worker at a nearby nursing home, regarding an 81-year-old woman who was terminally ill with a malignant brain tumor. However, it was the woman's husband the social worker was concerned about. This 78-year-old man was walking around with a suicide note in his jacket pocket, addressed to the police. I asked the social worker to ask the husband to call me. He did so immediately, in itself a positive prognostic sign.

"The social worker said I should call you," he said.

"She told me you are going through a very hard time," I replied.

"I've been through too much to live any more.," he said. "My wife . . ." He broke into bitter and uncontrollable sobs (which I did not hear from him again with such intensity until over a year of continued therapy).

Mr. V. was unable to continue talking; we therefore made an appointment for the next day. My tentative plan was to see him, establish further rapport, obtain some further information, and then hold the next meeting at his wife's bedside. Fate, however, intervened. Unknown to us, his wife was expiring during our call, and our meeting was postponed.

We made another appointment, but Mr. V. phoned back once again because he was ill with a virus. "I'm so sick, I feel I'm going to die," he said.

"Don't die until you see me," I said. That was a covert communication: "Don't die, I want you to live."

"That's funny," he responded, and I thought, "Any man who can laugh at my lousy humor is going to get better."

I rarely use humor at initial contacts, especially with a patient I have not yet seen, and most especially with someone in deep mourning, but it seemed appropriate.

Therapy was eventually initiated, and Mr. V. was seen as part of a comprehensive treatment program which included medication, the use of social service resources for his home, medical treatment, individual therapy, and group therapy. He was actually assigned to two groups at first: a bereavement group run by another member of the clinic, and the suicidal group run by myself.

His simultaneous membership in two groups at the same clinic was not a good idea, with a major complication being an enormous amount of splitting of the two therapists. We do not recommend such a procedure. On the other hand, individual therapy by one therapist and group therapy by another has been a more successful procedure, but the same therapist for both is still recommended.

In group therapy, Mr. V. was quite emotional and tearful. He was sometimes drunk, usually difficult, and persistently suicidal, but always involved with the group. He demonstrated at least the rudiments of the sense of humor indicated in our first contact. For example, one member of the group complained about always arguing with her brother who lived with her.

"Why don't you have an argument with me," Mr. V. suggested. "Then I'll get into a big temper and feel better."

Another example of his group interaction took place with 72-year-old Betsy N. Peter V. had been a member of the group for a year. Mrs. N had joined the group 2 months before, having reacted to a cancer operation with a psychotic depression and suicide attempt. Periodic hospitalizations extending over 2 years produced no improvement, but the hospital said they would no longer accept her. The operation had been a success and there was no evidence of cancer. However, she was anorexic and emaciated. The group had a very protective attitude towards her.

During this particular session, Mr. V. once again announced to the group that he felt very suicidal and hopeless, and intended to kill himself sooner or later.

Asked about hospitalization he firmly refused and said he would run away from the group and the hospital if I tried to hospitalize him. The group responses ranged widely, from, "Don't kill yourself, it's a sin;" to "You need to keep more active—go out more, join a senior center;" to an offer from one elderly woman to come to his apartment and straighten it out. Peter remained adamant in refusing all suggestions and insisting that he would kill himself.

I then turned to Mrs. N. and asked about her suicidal thoughts. Although almost mute and catatonic, she was the one who told Peter suicide was a sin. Nevertheless, she insisted that she was a burden to her entire family and needed to kill herself. She wanted to drive alone to the top of a high mountain and there take an overdose of pills.

Peter turned to her and with impressive, beautiful eloquence presented the reasons why she should live. He was completely convincing. He ended by declaring, "This does not apply to me." It was clear, however, that it did. Betsy, incidentally, eventually left the group at the insistence of her family, but follow-up telephone contacts indicated she is less suicidal and still alive.

Mr. V.'s multitude of medical as well as psychiatric symptoms required the entire staff to spend more time with him than with any other patient. Many of his complaints did not always ring true; and the group, which is usually solicitous of actively suicidal members, did not always take his suicidal ideation and threats seriously, although I did.

At one session, shortly after his exchange with Betsy N., he said, "And no matter what you say, I'm going to commit suicide by jumping out the window." The group responded with silence, except for one woman who said, "So why are you coming to therapy?" Mr. V. had no response.

I believe that the group was in tune with him. However, I made an appointment to see Mr. V. individually. He tearfully told me that he had opened his window and almost jumped, but at the last moment could not do so. He then burst into the convulsive sobs that I had first heard during our initial telephone contact.

This incident marked a turning point in Mr. V.'s treatment. He had said "no" to suicide, at least at that point. After that episode, he became significantly less suicidal, more socially active, less depressed, and less agitated.

Gender issues have come more to the forefront in recent times, but have not been studied in terms of treating the suicidal. The literature suggests women are more oriented toward feelings and relationships, while men are more reserved, cerebral, and less in touch with their feelings.

There was one experience where, by chance, only the four men in the group showed up, and not the four women. In that session, the men were much more open about their feelings and such issues as marital problems and sex than they had been in the mixed group.

Peter V., for example, confided that his wife wanted to have sex after she had been diagnosed with a brain tumor and he was unable to do so. Another patient said he had the same experience after his wife had a mastectomy.

Such experiences emphasize the importance of sex in the elderly and the potential value of sex therapy, especially in the face of physical illness.

There might be some value in studying the effect of homogeneous therapy groups for the suicidal consisting of all male and all female patients, comparing the results when the therapist is male or female or with mixed cotherapists, and comparing these in turn with the traditionally mixed but otherwise homogeneous groups.

THE HEALING POWER OF GROUPS

The central therapeutic influence of the group lies in a greater openness and sharing. Most elderly suicidal persons are private and secretive, carrying their self-destructive plans with them to the grave. I do not believe that the patients could have been so open or expressive or that their problems could have been dealt with as effectively, arousing such understanding and empathy, outside of a homogeneous group such as the one just described.

Group therapy helps the suicidal by providing an opportunity for social integration, something that is desperately needed by suicidal elderly persons. Most of them are lonely, even those who are married. They feel alienated and different from others. The homogeneous therapy group provides an opportunity for belonging, for helping others, for social cohesion, and to experience feelings of being understood and, in the process, to help themselves.

The group members developed a team spirit. They all knew what it is like to experience despair and hopelessness. At the same time, they were usually not actively suicidal or seriously depressed, and could therefore respond directly and empathically, but without becoming overwhelmed. they offered advice and shared their own thoughts, feelings, and experiences with similar problems. Most impressive was the degree to which the group members could empathize with and help contain each other's suicidal impulses.

The group was statistically at a high risk for suicide. Many were selected just because of the seriousness and extent of their self-destructive behavior and depressive symptoms. Several patients had to be hospitalized at psychiatric facilities at one time or another because of an exacerbation of depression or suicidal impulses. Three were placed in nursing homes or similar institutions because their physical or psychiatric condition deteriorated. One implication is that continued monitoring of the medical and nutritional state of these patients is necessary in addition to the symptoms and problems more directly related to depression and suicide.

The group was a very positive experience for the majority of its members. Improved social and interpersonal functioning were seen in these lonely and alienated individuals, and a greater sense of community. Group members joined or resumed contacts with senior centers and similar activities. Some became closer to their families.

The group is a place where what is usually considered secret and shameful can be expressed openly, with a resulting marked decrease in feelings of stigma and shame.

In choosing the group members some intangibles were involved, such as the fit between different participants. An effective selection process is necessary because they need to be compatible and capable of working with each other. The support of the social and family network is also important. In patients who did not improve, the opposition of the relatives often played a manifest role. In those who did respond, the family was cooperative, despite the presence at times of severe family pathology. Availability and cooperativeness are not always a function of good adjustment.

Homogeneous group therapy was actually less strenuous for me than seeing the patients individually, especially because of the perceptiveness and natural skill of the group members. They did a better job than I could alone, and with time my respect for their strength and wisdom has increased.

Most of the members of the geriatric group had a good sense of humor, and they were the ones who improved. Those deficient in a sense of humor did not improve. For example, Florence R., a periodically depressed woman, entered the room attractively dressed and made up. "You're looking good," commented one woman.

"Nothing like a coat of paint for an old barn," replied Florence.

Ann, a chronically depressed woman asked the group, "Who do you think will be running for President? (This was early in 1988, before the presidential candidates had been chosen.) "As long as he's not from Hollywood," replied Bertha, a depressed woman with a chronic dementia!

Mary, a 73-year-old woman, asked what psychoanalysis was.

I explained that the patient lies on a couch and says whatever comes to her mind.

"She says whatever comes to her mind?" Mary repeated, in surprise.

"That's true," I said, and then turned to the others. "What do you do when you lie on a couch?" I asked.

"None of your business," replied Florence.

Need I add that Florence was one of those who improved?

The group members tended to convene early and talk among themselves until the session began. The sessions were often lively, even more so before I arrived. It was then that the group members talked a great deal and confided to each other about ailments or family relationships. At such times laughter was frequent. As I walked toward the group therapy room one morning to begin a session, their laughter rang out, and a colleague said "I see your suicidal group is here."

7

Individual
Psychotherapy

The basic principles of psychotherapy with the suicidal elderly were presented in Chapter 4 on "The Healing Relationship," while its applications to crisis intervention, family therapy, and group psychotherapy were discussed in Chapters 3, 5, and 6. What was said there also applies to individual therapy with the suicidal. In addition the integration of individual treatment with family therapy has been recommended by several authorities. These include Zimmerman and La Sorsa (1992) with adolescents, and in the treatment of the suicidal elderly by this author.

HOMAGE TO THE INDIVIDUAL

Individual treatment is still the most frequently utilized form of psychotherapy, its popularity undiminished despite the proliferation of biologically-oriented interventions. Its persistence may be a tribute to our American heritage, where the individual is celebrated, as Whitman sang and Hawthorne wrote. Walt Whitman wrote "Song of Myself"—it would not have seemed quite right for him to have written "Song of Ourselves."

The honor accorded to individuality was also expressed by Hawthorne in *The House of Seven Gables*, where the author expressed his admiration of the hero, Holgrave, who possessed "the rare and high quality of reverence for another's individuality." This chapter, therefore, is dedicated to the American Individual, with a reminder that autonomy can only flourish in a state of social cohesion.

These literary statements have implications for therapy. Hawthorne implied that the reverence for individuality is an affirmation of each individual. Such affirmation further implies a refusal to permit one person to control or hold power over other people, but rather to esteem and strive to understand each one of them. That quality is also a basic tenet in all humanistic psychotherapy. Unconditional acceptance, warmth, and accurate empathy are among the qualities of the successful therapist (Truax & Carkhuf, 1967).

Several schools of therapy have been designed expressly for the individual treatment of depressed patients. These include the cognitive behavior therapy of Beck and his colleagues (1979), and the interpersonal therapy of Klerman and colleagues (1984). Their procedures can be applied to suicidal people of all ages. The essence of their contribution to the treatment described in this book has been summarized in Chapter 5 on the commonalities of all therapy.

There have been two forms of treatment that have been developed specifically for the suicidal. One is the "ego vulnerability" model of the Menninger school (Smith & Eyman, 1988), presumably for all ages. The other is the "narcissistic vulnerability" model of Maltsberger (1991), specifically for the suicidal elderly. Both are psychoanalytically oriented.

THE "NARCISSISTIC VULNERABILITY" MODEL

Maltsberger makes a variety of theoretical points followed by the treatment implications. The major one is that the elderly suicidal person is unable to maintain an adequate sense of self, of self-esteem, or a sense of reality when left alone. As a result, they are vulnerable to profound feelings of worthlessness, "annihilatory anxiety," and panic which can lead to suicide.

The recommendations that follow are that treatment must often begin in a safe or sheltered setting such as a psychiatric ward, and that electroconvulsive therapy is often preferable to medication. The next point is that a therapeutic relationship can be developed and treatment continued after discharge. The third point is that continued therapy is required.

The formulation emphasizes the inability of the suicidal person to function without the help or support of others. Therefore, Maltsberger believes that what can be done with the suicidal elderly is limited. Supportive therapy must be utilized to provide the patient with the functions he or she cannot perform alone.

Conroy (1990) criticizes Maltsberger for this negative, deficit oriented view of the suicidal. At least as described. It appears as though people are either completely dependent upon others or completely independent.

However, in the description of his treatment, Maltsberger emerges with much warmth, kindliness, and a positive approach. He recognizes the importance of promoting the grief process, and of course presents much wise advice for dealing with the therapist's countertransference. Finally, Maltsberger emphasizes the importance of the availability of the therapist, and the value of involving elderly suicidal patients in support groups and other activities.

THE "EGO VULNERABILITY" MODEL

The Menninger model conceptualizes suicide as based upon three conditions: A fragile or disturbed identity, an event that threatens the identity, and deficits in managing affect and in solving problems.

The therapeutic implications involve helping patients become aware of their self destructive and self punitive wishes. The basis of these urges rest upon their conviction that they do not deserve success on the one hand. On the other hand, they expect to be magically nurtured by people who know their needs and fulfill them unconditionally. "These individuals seemed to be searching for an all-powerful, perfectly attuned mother who would supply them with endless comfort and gratification, and who could help them recapture the pleasures of infancy and the feelings of completeness and oneness" (Richman & Eyeman, 1990, p. 142). But they were also very ambivalent and fearful of the depriving and critical bad mother.

Smith and Eyeman (1988) recognize the difficulties in expressing affect that is so characteristic of the suicidal. Their treatment consists of exploring situations of anger and strengthening adapting coping devices. When the patient is in a suicidal crisis, says Eyeman, part of the therapy consists of presenting alternatives to their belief that suicide is the only solution. As does Maltsberger, as well as everyone who has worked intensively to treat the suicidal, they recognize that the therapist may become the recipient of intense anger.

One of the most important contributions of the Menninger model is their presentation of therapy as providing a safe "holding environment," a concept derived from Winnicott (1965), where the therapist is like a good parent who is protective and nurturing but also sets realistic limits.

This is the need for mothering which I have seen over and over in my practice as the overriding need of both the suicidal patient and the entire family. In my experience a holding environment for the elderly suicidal patient contains three major aspects: First, the therapist becomes a good parent figure for the suicidal individual; second, the therapist is a good parent for the entire family, for all the members are suffering from great feelings of early deprivation and the need for mothering; and thirdly, the therapist affirms and renews the developmental tasks of competence, initiative, industry, dealing with lost relationships, cultivating new friendships, and reinforcing the person's continued active membership in the family.

The Menninger model emphasizes that the therapist must help the patient to "appropriately grieve and mourn the loss" "(Richman & Eyeman, 1990, p. 144). Thus the "narcissistic vulnerability" and "ego vulnerability" models and certainly my integrative therapy all emphasize the importance of facilitating the grief process. In all three models, the therapist is a warm, accessible, and understanding human being who accepts and empathizes with the needs and wishes of the patient. While all of these are influenced by psychoanalytic theory and therapy, they incorporated the findings from a wide variety of disciplines and have thus enriched and advanced the effective treatment of suicidal people.

THE INDIVIDUAL IN CONTEXT

Respect for the individual does not mean seeing the person apart from his or her family and social context. Furst and Ostow (1965) overstated the case when they presented their psychoanalytic view that "suicide is a highly *individual, personal act* [authors' italics'] . . . as such, it can be accounted for *only* [italics added] in terms of intrapsychic events that constitute the essential, final pathway to the suicidal act" (p. 190).

Such a dichotomy between the individual and everything else can *only* be considered a limitation of the authors, which is contradicted by their own accounts. For example, they tell the following story: "A patient who had lost his father, grandfather, and two brothers by suicide and was himself suicidal reported the suicide of yet another brother with the terse remark, 'This is the way we do it'" (p. 194). This patient's "we" could not have referred to a purely "individual, personal" act. Furst and Ostow could have acknowledged that such examples suggest suicide is not *only* an individual event.

The context can influence directly whether a suicidal act will occur. Steiner (1967), in his account of life in the concentration camp Treblinka, described how inmates would commit suicide, usually by hanging, with the help of compassionate other inmates. However, the camp prisoners planned a revolt, and at that point they discouraged suicides. The suicides ceased.

A psychoanalytic view is completely compatible with a comprehensive approach. Nevertheless, I have never seen or heard of a suicide which was entirely an individual, personal act. To see it as such can be hazardous to successful treatment.

For example, the usual healing qualities of individual therapy can pose a major danger for the suicidal. These qualities include the ability to form a mature and intimate interpersonal relationship, and the encouragement of the unfolding of growth, competence, and self-esteem. These become dangers when the resulting implications of autonomy and a change in the relationship between the patient and other family members pose a *perception* of threat to the very existence of the the family system. Growth and increased autonomy can rarely be one-sided.

The family members, therefore, take measures to protect its integrity. Conflict develops between the patient and family, with the outcome being the ubiquitous negative therapeutic reaction, where the result of success is failure.

Florence C. was a 65-year-old widow who entered therapy with the chief complaints of depression, suicidal thoughts, and great discord in the relationship with her 30-year-old daughter. Many of the conflicts revolved around old resentments by the daughter because of how she was treated as a child. Mrs. C. was seen in individual therapy, where she quickly formed a very positive transference and working alliance. Her depression lifted and she spoke to her daughter about wishes to work out their conflicts.

Both her daughter and her boyfriend reacted by ridiculing Mrs. C. for "having a boyfriend," meaning the therapist. The patient reacted with a recurrence of her depression, complaints that the therapist was not helpful, and eventually by discontinuing treatment.

Nevertheless, individual therapy has been successful with the majority of elderly suicidal persons who enter treatment. Unfortunately, not enough people know of this power of psychotherapy. In fact, there is an unfortunate tendency in the literature to consider the older suicidal person unsuitable. The extent of the problem, which is based upon ageism and ignorance within the professional community, its historical roots, and its remedy through proper training and education, has been presented earlier in this work.

Psychoanalysis has tended to treat younger patients. Kahana (1979) pointed out that when Freud said psychoanalysis was not suitable for persons older than 50, the average life expectancy was about 40. In the light of the great increase in the life span as well as changes in psychoanalytic practice, Freud's view is no longer tenable.

Reported cases of psychoanalysis or even psychotherapy with the suicidal elderly are infrequent, although there are descriptions of psychotherapy of elderly patients who are severely disturbed. Segal (1958), for example, treated a man in his seventies suffering from depression and paranoia.

Kahana described the successful psychotherapy of a woman in her seventies with a severe agitated depression and paranoia, who was also placed on anti-depressant medication. The effects of her treatment have wider implications for the treatment of the elderly. "Upon recovery," said Kahana, "she began to assist older, infirm" residents in the nursing home.

Kahana saw her actions as "reparation for having been such a burden." However, her basically appropriate and adaptive behavior of helping others touches upon the place of Adler's description of "social interest" as an index of maturity and adjustment, along with the more customary objectives of increasing individual competence and social cohesiveness. The adaptive value of helping others is one of the major reasons for recommending the use of the elderly to help the elderly. What is ethical most often fosters ego integrity and the affirmation of a meaningful life.

Of all the advantages of individual psychotherapy, what has impressed therapists the most is "the opportunity for the older person to develop an intimate relationship that would seem to be highly desirable for the elderly (Mcmordie & Blom, 1979, p. 163).

Harriet S. is an 85-year-old widow who presented with the chief complaint of having cancer. She had had intestinal polyps removed which were precancerous, but there had been no evidence of an active malignancy. She refused to leave her house; she suffered from chronic depression and social withdrawal, marked dissatisfaction and conflict with her children, and suicidal threats.

With difficulty, a family interview was arranged with her three sons, but they lived in different areas and no further appointments could be scheduled. Mrs. S. refused group therapy. Her treatment consisted basically of individual psychotherapy, with anti-depressant medication and occasional interviews with the geriatric psychiatrist.

A major positive influence was her internist who had referred her to the clinic. When in a depressive or suicidal crisis, which was moderately frequent, she felt free to call her psychotherapist. She also called her internist almost as often. Her greatest social support, however, was the internist's receptionist who served as a willing ear and an endless fountain of advice.

Her belief that she had cancer quickly subsided and it became clear that she was a very bright, responsive woman with a capacity to form warm interpersonal relationships. However, she was filled with resentment at the emptiness of her life and at what she saw as the turning away from her by her children. She established a strong and erotic relationship with the therapist, but it did not generalize outside the treatment situation. She continued to limit her activities primarily to watching television while lying in bed.

Mrs. S's therapy can be considered an example of the value of brief, problem solving treatment. She was especially vulnerable to loss, and reacted to such events with a depressive withdrawal. During therapy a friend she had known for over 50 years died. She became more seclusive, together with an exacerbation of angry and depressive thoughts.

Several months after treatment began, the therapist left the clinic. She again experienced a resurgence of her somatic symptoms and complaints about her children. Dealing with separation became the major topic of the sessions for the last 3 months of treatment. Finally, she transferred and expanded her activities from therapists to the outside. She established new relationships with her next door neighbors, and took special delight in observing and playing with their little grandchildren.

The "Myth of Exclusiveness," the belief that the formation of a new intimate relationship can only be achieved at the cost of ending an existing older one, is particularly prominent in individual therapy, with its one-to-one approach. The myth is persistent and impervious to words or explanations. It must be accepted. Nevertheless, it can be modified.

Sophie M. was a 67-year-old widow seen in individual therapy preceded by one family session. She lived alone, isolated from her sisters and brother yet dominated by the family rules and expectations. Her siblings complained about the relationships she had established, insisting they were bad influences. She had one close friend in particular who she felt she had to give up. Her therapist suggested that she tell her family about this acquaintance but that she be very casual as well as critical of this friend emphasizing how unimportant she was. However, she was to bring her friend to meet her family once in a while. Her sisters liked and even approved of this woman, and criticized Sophie for not being more friendly.

Even the myth of exclusiveness can be modified if the threat to older relationships can be diminished or removed.

In my own work, individual therapy is integrated with a treatment plan. Its proper utilization depends upon the nature of the situation.

Catherine E., aged 74, had a lengthy history of depressive episodes with suicidal ideation following the death of her 35-year-old son. She would be hospitalized until her condition cleared, then discharged, but with inadequate and insufficient follow-up until the next episode. The cycle would then be repeated.

She was finally referred for outpatient therapy, where she was treated with medication, and supportive group therapy, which was initially biweekly and then monthly. She responded very positively to the treatment with no depressive episodes and a more active social and family life.

Individual sessions were available upon request. For example, she phoned one day and requested an individual meeting, after losing the tip of a finger in an accident.. The therapist saw her immediately, the following day. She said that in the past she would have a breakdown following such events, but this time she was fine. She and the therapist agreed that her precaution in requesting an extra session was sensible. It demonstrated to her that care was available, but was not otherwise needed.

The therapeutic result in this example was based upon the evidence of a secure and reliable relationship with a trustworthy and available therapist.

Individual psychotherapy within the context of family and other therapies is called for in helping the elderly deal with developmentally earlier tasks such as initiative and the use of their abilities. With chronically depressed persons whose life role is that of the helpless patient, the cultivation of competence is best dealt with in individual sessions. These often involve direct coaching and practice during the sessions in the use and application of their skills in the activities of daily living and in family and social activities. The success of these efforts often means that the therapist must anticipate and be prepared to deal with the negative therapeutic reaction in the family.

While individual psychotherapy may be widely practiced, it is rarely sufficient in and of itself. As Toolan (1984) emphasized in his discussion of the suicidal child, parents must always be included in the treatment plan. He believed, rightfully, that the same therapist should treat both.

Toolan's view applies at all ages when treating the suicidal, in that the family must always be included. With very few of the elderly, of course, does that include the parents. When parents are available, however, they should be included, even if in a nursing home, along with children and the other family members.

In summary, individual therapy permits an intimate relationship outside the family, with an opportunity to remain actively engaged, to cultivate activities and success, and widen one's personal and social horizons while maintaining family cohension. To succeed in this endeavor the therapist must see that the treatment does not conflict with the family loyalties of the patient. That is why a family session early in the treatment program is necessary, even when individual therapy is the treatment of choice. Individual psychotherapy has and will continue to have an honored place in the treatment of suicide.

Epilogue

"... You see backward through time, and you feel the flow of time, and realize that you're only part of a great endless procession."

—John Huston (In Hendrickson, 1990, p. 121)

This book has presented the research and especially the clinical findings on elderly suicide, and the steps required to evaluate and overcome self-destruction. The methods for achieving these goals may differ, but each treatment modality offers something valuable; therefore, a multi-level, multi-disciplinary approach is most effective. Each suicidal person is to be understood in his or her biopsychosocial uniqueness, and a comprehensive treatment plan devised which takes the individual and the situation into account.

The therapy that is selected depends upon the training, experience, and personal comfort of the therapist, but all treatment of suicide begins with crisis intervention. When someone is already in therapy and a suicidal crisis arises, it is as though treatment has just begun and the therapist would switch to crisis intervention. The same principles apply to patients in psychoanalysis, family therapy, group therapy, behavior therapy, interpersonal therapy, medication therapy and so forth.

My recommendation is to bring in the family, because family crisis intervention is most effective for acutely suicidal persons. That is why it is essential to have a family meeting at the beginning of therapy, no matter what the modality. That applies to biologically oriented therapy as well as psychotherapy. Once the crisis is resolved, the therapist may wish to resume the earlier approach.

156

The key is flexibility, empathy, and a willingness to confront extreme emotions. The therapist must be in touch with the wealth and turmoil of feelings and reactions, which in their sum can be understood through the concepts of transference and countertransference.

The social equation must simultaneously be considered, especially the nature and extent of the person's support systems and the social and medical resources that are available. In other words, treatment of the suicidal elderly brings the interdependence of peoples and generations into sharp focus. The future of effective suicide prevention lies in three areas: clinical practice, objective research, the alleviation of social ills, and the harmonious integration of all three.

We have impressive models for such work. The integration of research and practice has been the basis of the behavioral and cognitive therapies (Beck, Rush, Shaw, & Emery, 1979), and interpersonal therapy (Klerman et al., 1984). Carl Rogers (1942) pioneered the public perusal of psychotherapy sessions 50 years ago.

More sophisticated procedures have been applied to psychoanalytically oriented therapy by Luborsky and his coworkers (1984), and the Mt. Zion Hospital group in San Francisco (Weiss, Sampson, et al., 1986). Clinical research is beginning to address the treatment of elderly depression (Ferguson, 1991) but has been limited largely to individual therapy and non-suicidal patients. Research is now needed on the treatment of suicidal persons, including group and family therapies as well as individual.

THE FUTURE OF LATE LIFE SUICIDE

Old age is traditionally a time to relax and reap the fruits of a lifetime of labor. Today, with Social Security, Medicare, and other buffers against want and insecurity, the aged have never had it so good. Studies of the elderly generally report the presence of high morale and satisfaction in living (Ryff, 1989).

Future trends include the continued lengthening of the life span, greater opportunities to remain active, the maintenance of good physical health with a longer period of independence, self-care, and the continuation of high morale and life satisfaction.

On the negative side there is the inevitable decline associated with aging, the need for more health care providers, and the increased drain upon Social Security and other services, which have to be paid for by younger generations.

This last concern has been the basis for biased diatribes against social measures to help the elderly. The recommended remedies range from taking monies used for Social Security to help children in need, denying medical care to the elderly unless they are rich, to legal measures for helping the elderly commit suicide. These suggestions are all based upon the presence of a deficit economy with expectations that the 21st will also be a deficit century. But it need not be so. The challenge is to transform this age of diminished expectations into an era of expanding horizons.

The accompanying challenge is for the young and old to work together for their mutual benefit. The social problems of the elderly can be dealt with without placing the generations into conflict. What helps one generation can help all generations. Helping the elderly can have a most salutary effect upon all ages. Whatever enhances growth at one age enriches life at another. As we have seen, the roles and relationships of one person are inseparable from the roles and relationships of significant people in the family system and social network. Therefore one of the best ways to prevent suicide in the young is to prevent suicide in the old.

This is not to deny the barriers to successful aging, especially for those who become suicidal. The majority of suicidal elderly persons suffer from a variety of ailments and vicissitudes. Many of these are also present in younger suicidal persons, but they are more severe and of a longer duration in the elderly. To paraphrase Schuckman (1975), overcoming elderly suicide is not for sissies; it takes strength to age and to overcome adversity successfully. These strengths have been overlooked by many writers, but not all.

Erikson (1950) saw the success or failure of aging as based upon how the individual dealt with the age-related developmental tasks and crises throughout the life span. Gitelson (1975), in contrast, described normal aging in terms that resembled psychopathology. His application of psychoanalysis became a source of negative judgments, while Erikson's formulations led to an expansion of psychoanalytic developmental theory. This book accepts the insights of Erikson, whose life span approach to aging combines both Freud and Durkheim, the social and the psychological.

Many elderly persons whose morale and life satisfaction remain high are subject to the same biological, social, and personal ills, but do not succumb to despair and suicide. Differences between affirmation versus disconfirmation of life are found in the acceptability of suicide as a solution versus the acceptability of life, the nature of the person's value system versus the nihilistic rejection of values, and the degree of engagement in life despite adversity.

Ida, an 85-year-old woman, her body disabled by a stroke and confined to a wheelchair was bemoaning her fate. She lived in a nursing home and had had to give up a beautiful home. She was a widow who missed her husband; her children who lived hundreds and thousands of miles away were rarely able to visit her.

"Do you think you might be better off dead?" I asked.

She looked at me, astonished. "The very idea!" "What, be buried in the ground," she said, "I have time for that."

I met Ida when visiting a cousin in the same nursing home. She would wheel herself over and we would chat. Recognizing my interest and positive response to humor, she usually greeted me with a joke from her extensive repertoire.

The person who retains his or her sense of humor is not ready for death and certainly not for suicide. That is true, even on one's deathbed.

Oliver Perry Allen was usually known as "Opie" by his friends and family. Living in the mid–1800s, he had acquired a reputation as an inveterate punster, which he retained to the end. When he became seriously ill and was lying on his deathbed, he was in great pain, and the doctor had given him a sedative. The relatives gathered around his bedside, and one explained to the other that he had been administered an opiate. Opie opened his eyes and weakly gasped, "Yes, that's what Opie ate."

Shortly after, he died, and has been remembered fondly through the generations for retaining his humor to the very end. Humor is a better legacy than suicide.

Humor is one of the many assets of the elderly, together with knowledge, understanding, empathy, and wisdom. Assets refer to those qualities of the suicidal elderly which make recovery and effective living possible. They are the same assets as those present in all the elderly who maintain high morale and much satisfaction in life. Their resources include a refusal to accept suicide as a solution and to search for life-affirming alternatives, as was true of Ida. Implicitly, too, assets include an awareness, at some level, of positive qualities in the self.

The psychotherapies that have been presented in this book rely upon the positive qualities of the emotionally distressed elderly, combined with affirming the self and others, leading to social cohesion and social interest. Add to these the availability of a family and other support systems, including medical and other professional resources, and the treatment of the suicidal elderly becomes realistically hopeful. With the discovery of how much the elderly have to offer, the therapist, too, grows in wisdom, knowledge, understanding, and strength.

THE LIVING WILL AND THE WILL TO LIVE

The euthanasia movement advocates that the time and nature of a person's death is his or hers to decide, as well as a matter between the patient and the doctor. The doctor must be prepared and knowledgeable about such matters, although there is a question of how many are suited by training, experience, and personal inclination to deal with death as well as life.

Dr. Leonard Kahn and myself (Richman & Kahn, 1986) once studied the attitudes of physicians and other health professionals towards the suicides of doctors, and the implications for medical school teaching and post-graduate education. We found a general consensus that education and training in suicide prevention was too little, too late, too superficial, lacking in continuity, and that further training was needed at all levels.

Doctors have saved many lives, and inevitably have encountered many deaths, but they must not abdicate their healing role simply because the patient is ill, old, and may not live. The same values must apply to suicide. Doctors cannot save every despairing suicidal or self-destructive patient who comes to the office or clinic, but the health professional cannot avoid such a person. The majority of those who commit suicide have seen a physician shortly before their act. All the evidence therefore points to the responsibility of the doctor to recognize when a patient may be suicidal, including how to deal with the situation and knowing when and how to refer.

There are opposing arguments that suicide is none of medicine's business and that the prevention of suicide is an infringement of human rights. Szasz (1986) has argued that physicians are not qualified by their training or values to deal with suicide. Besides, suicide is a right and not something to be forcibly prevented. After all, is not a person's life his or her own, to do with as he or she wills?

Jerome Beatty (1964) told a story about an old man who was lying on his deathbed. He called in his relatives and said to them, "I'm dying. My time has come. The question is, what shall we tell the doctor?"

"Don't tell him," said his relatives. "It would upset him too much." The general consensus was that it would be cruel for seriously ill people to discuss death with their doctor.

Beatty's humor seems to confirm Szasz's point that doctors cannot deal with death. The trouble is that suicidal patients have not read Szasz and continue to visit their physicians in large numbers. That is only one among the many reasons for physicians to be involved in learning more about suicide. Another "trouble" is that educating physicians in recognizing and treating depression and suicide has demonstrably decreased the suicide rate (Rutz et al., 1989).

There are five other major considerations for anyone confronted with a suicidal person to keep in mind:

1) The suicidal person is markedly ambivalent about living and dying, and often welcomes those on the side of life.
2) The suicidal state is usually time limited and runs its course, after which the person is no longer suicidal and glad to be alive.
3) The act often takes place in a dissociated or altered state of consciousness when the person is almost literally not himself.
4) The suicidal despair is more often based upon relationships and other problems in living than wishes for dying, even in those who are terminally ill.
5) The role of others in the person's life and death is prominent, including the wish by significant others that the person live, and the realization that one's existence is valued by others.

The positive and reaching out attitude of health and mental health professionals is a crucial part of the treatment process. Chief among these attitudes is hopefulness and a refusal to give up on life, rather than a surrender to disgust and despair. As Payne (1975) said, the recognition by a doctor that a patient is considering suicide, and the doctor's wish to prevent that act, may be crucial in preserving the patient's wish to live. Of course, the power of the life wish applies to all those in meaningful contact with the suicidal.

Such reflections apply throughout the life span. I described a 90-year-old man who was hospitalized following a suicide attempt (Richman, 1986). He was happy that he did not succeed, and declared that he felt as though he were first starting to live.

The experience of this 90-year-old paralleled the experience of Arthur Rubenstein at age 19, following his suicide attempt (Rubenstein, 1973). Those who are saved, even from the most genuine self-destructive acts, are generally pleased and grateful.

The suicidal person's ambivalence, hope struggling with despair, the forces of life, and the importance of others, may all coalesce in the one last visit to the doctor. That visit may represent an unspoken appeal for help before going on to the final and irrevocable act. A knowledge of suicide is therefore important for the physician. He cannot avoid the suicidal person, but he must make a choice about what to do with him or for him. Many of those who kill themselves use the pills and medicines given to them by a physician.

Psychiatric centers, hospitals, mental hygiene clinics, the telephone hot lines, and other crisis services primarily serve those who come actively seeking help. Many elderly suicidal persons do not do so; public services and agencies do not reach the most suicidal old people. The one person that does is the physician.

The doctor, too, may need help and guidance in these matters, and may need that help quickly. Special consultation services for health professionals are urgently needed. I recommend that a suicide hot line be established, offering a special service for physicians and other health professionals, who can call for an instant consultation when faced with a suicidal or severely emotionally disturbed patient. A central requirement for the professional working with suicidal patients is the availability of people to whom he can turn (Richman, 1986).

Suicide poses a special challenge to the medical and mental health professionals. To help the suicidal elderly, the therapist must first look within at his or her own anxiety about suicide and socially conditioned attitudes about aging. John Rosen (1970) said that the problem of suicide makes us all our brother's keeper. That is the broader foundation. Commitment to one person touches upon the brotherhood of all mankind.

TOWARD THE 21ST CENTURY

Suicide is one of the outcomes of poor morale and low life satisfaction. There are other possible outcomes, of course. In those suffering from ill-being, whatever the form it assumes, the goal of treatment or counseling is to restore a state of well-being. This is a view which is achieving world-wide acceptance.

The 1989 Conference of the World Federation for Mental Health in Luxor, Egypt, drafted a "Declaration of Human Rights for the Mentally Ill." They adopted the definition of health of the World Health Organization: "a state of complete physical, mental, social, and moral well-being." That comprehensive definition is the one accepted here as the goal of our therapeutic efforts with the elderly suicidal person.

The life-affirming treatment of the suicidal elderly also makes a social statement. This is a death dealing world where violence and terrorism against the innocent has been part of social policy. At the same time, this is an age of medical and biological miracles, where people can live better lives than ever before.

It is between these two forces, the life expanding and the life destructive, that the movement to permit and encourage suicide, especially in the elderly, has grown. It is a misplaced use of energies on the part of the proponents to fight for the legalization of physician assisted suicides, while doing nothing to alleviate the conditions associated with elderly suicide. We must exert greater efforts to deal with the destructive forces of all kinds that are being unleashed in the world. I consider the struggle to prevent suicide in the elderly part of the striving to prevent all self-inflicted and other-inflicted man-made disasters.

A promising development is the growth of the self-help movement, which has a long and honorable history in this country. When immigrants arrived in America, they set up self-help organizations to help those in need. I recommend that the elderly carry on that tradition. The best direction for the future is for the well elderly to help the feeble or impaired elderly. Those who have remained healthy and active in old age are obligated to help their fellows who have fared less well. Peer help is recommended because the bell tolls for all of us.

The success of peer involvement is contingent upon an adequate selection and screening process, followed by competency-based training and adequate remuneration. Such measures will reduce the burden on the younger population, and reassure them that they, too, can look forward to a socially civilized and personally comfortable old age.

What, then, of the future? Extrapolating from current medical, social, and general treatment trends, changes will take place in the nature of the future elderly population. Many of the vicissitudes of the aging process will remain the same, based as they are upon the enduring developmental tasks of the last stages of life. Loss and separation, especially death of a spouse will continue to be predominant areas of stress. Other enduring problems will include retirement, and the need to cope with status, income, self-esteem and other losses. Changes in roles over the life span, loss of health, and coping with physical and mental decline will continue.

If the elderly help the elderly, such problems will be dealt with more competently, empathically, and compassionately. However, those with the greatest difficulty in coming to terms with aging and death will continue to experience great problems in the 21st Century, as they do today.

Because of what we have learned and are learning about the danger signs of suicidal potential, combined with the advances in biological, psychological, and social forms of treatment, more will be accomplished in the future to deal effectively with the physical, emotional, and social challenges of aging. With the greater intellectual sophistication and psychological mindness of future cohorts, there will be a greater acceptance of counseling and psychotherapy.

But the future is always just a moment away. If we are to reduce elderly suicide in the future, the time to start is now, by confronting and overcoming the conditions that prevent us from rejecting death and from choosing life. Both the older and the younger generations must examine their ageist and other prejudices more objectively. Medical advances are not the enemy. Whether the biochemical revolution is a blessing or a curse depends upon what we make of it. Continued advances in the biological and physical therapies of depression and other conditions related to suicide can be a great blessing.

Human nature is stable and there is more continuity than discontinuity in development throughout life (Costa & McCrae, 1990). Nevertheless, the elderly of the future will not be the same as the elderly of today. The social milieu and professional services will be different. The attitudes of professionals will be more positive.

The literature on the suicidal elderly has mistakenly presented their suicidal state as less dynamic and less interpersonal than that of the younger person. Psychotherapy is either not mentioned or presented as counterindicated. The treatment is physical (ECT), biochemical (drugs), and environmental (placement in a nursing home or some other institution). Such treatment attitudes are going to change.

These predictions are based solidly upon clinical work with the elderly in the context of biochemical studies of suicidal behavior, social studies of demographic trends, and epidemiological investigations of the effects of changes and improvements in medical practice. The future, I predict, will continue the advances in understanding of biochemical and brain behaviors, their effects upon the entire organism, and the maintenance of physical health and cognitive abilities.

There will be a greater awareness and appreciation of the value of psychotherapy with older suicidal persons. Therapy will become more of a collaboration between the therapist and the patient, and will take place throughout the life span, which by the mid-21st century will have reached an average age of over a hundred. More of the elderly will be involved as both therapists and patients.

The study of aging is still a young science; helping people to age successfully and to present elderly suicides is still a young art. We are just beginning to learn.

In the future, life extension will have greater positive implications than it has now, with less anxiety and insecurity. The recommendation, then, is to stick around, for there will be many reasons to stay alive.

References

Abend, S. M. (1989). Countertransference and psychoanalytic technique.. *Psychoanalytic Quarterly, 58*, 374–393.

Abraham, K. (1953). The applicability of psycho-analytic treatment to patients at an advanced age. In *Selected papers* (original work published 1919), pp. 312–317. New York: Basic Books.

Adamic, L. (1942). In: Burnett, W. (Ed.) *This is my best.* New York: Dial.

Akiskal, H. S. (1991). Diagnosis and clinical management of difficult-to-treat affective disorders. *Psychiatric Letter, 3*, Fair Oaks Hospital, N. J.

Alexander, F., & French, T. M. (1945). *Psychoanalytic psychotherapy.* New York: Ronald Press.

Allen, T. E. (1967). Suicidal impulse in depression and paranoia. *International Journal of Psycho-Analysis, 46*, 433–438.

Bachrach, S. J. (1951). Some factors in the prediction of suicide. *Neuropsychiatry, 1*, 21–27.

Bassuk, E. L., & Birk, A. W. (1984). *Emergency psychiatry: Concepts, methods, and practices.* New York: Plenum.

Bateson, G., Jackson, D. D., Haley, J., & Weakland, J. (1956). Towards a theory of schizophrenia. *Behavioral Science, 1*, 251–264.

Beatty, J. (1964). *One o'clock in the button factory.* New York: Macmillan.

Beck, A. T., Rush, A. J., Shaw, B. R., & Emery, G. (1979). *Cognitive therapy of depression.* New York: Guilford.

Berne, E. (1964). *Games people play.* New York: Grove Press.

Berman, A. L. (Ed.) (1990). *Suicide prevention: Case consultations.* New York: Springer Publishing Co.

Berman, A. L., & Jobes, D. A. (1991). *Adolescent suicide: Assessment and intervention.* Washington, D. C.: American Psychological Assn.

Billings, J. H., Rosen, D. H., Asimos, C., & Motto, J. A. (1974). Observations on long-term group therapy with suicidal and depressed persons. *Life Threatening Behavior, 4* (3), 160–170.

165

Binswanger, L. (1958). The case of Ellen West, anathropological–clinical study. In: R. May, E. Angel, & H. F. Ellenberger, (Eds.) *Existence. A new dimension in psychiatry and psychology.* pp. 237–364. New York: Basic Books.

Bloom, M., Duchon, E., Frires, G., Hanson, H., Hurd, G., & South, V. (1971). *The Gerontologist (Winter, Part 1),* 11, 292–299.

Bloom, V. (1967). An analysis of suicide at a training center. *American Journal of Psychiatry, 123,* 918–925.

Bock, E. W., & Webber, I. L. (1972). Suicide among the elderly: Isolating widowhood and mitigating alternatives. *Journal of Marriage and the Family, 34,* 24–31.

Boldt, M. (1982). Normative evaluations of suicide and death. *Omega, 13* (2), 145–157.

Boldt, M. (1987). Defining suicide: Implications for suicide behavior and for suicide prevention. *Crisis, 8* (1), 3–13.

Bongar, B. (1991). *The suicidal patient. Clinical and legal standards of care.* Washington, DC: American Psychological Association.

Boss, M. (1963). *Psychoanalysis and daseinanalysis.* New York: Basic Books.

Boss, P. E., Caron, W., Horbal, J., & Mortimer, J. (1990). Predictors of depression in caregivers of dementia patients: Boundary ambiguity and mastery. *Family Process, 29* (3), 245–254.

Boszormenyi-Nagy, I., & Spark, G. M. (1973). *Invisible loyalties: Reciprocity in intergenerational family therapy.* New York: Harper & Row.

Bowen, M. (1978). *Family therapy in clinical practice.* New York: Jason Aronson.

Bowers, M. K., Mullan, H., & Berkowitz, B. (1959). Observations on suicide occurring during group psychotherapy. *American Journal of Psychotherapy, 13,* 93–106.

Bowlby, J. (1969). *Attachment and loss. Vol. I: Attachment. New York: Basic Books.*

Bowlby, J. (1973). *Attachment and loss. Vol. II: Separation.* New York: Basic Books.

Breggin, P. R. (1991). *Toxic medicine: Why therapy, empathy, and love must replace the drugs, electroshock, and biochemical theories of the "new psychiatry."* New York: St. Martin's Press.

Brown, G. W., & Harris, T. O. (Eds.) (1991). The meaning of stress. *Contemporary Psychology, 36,* 113.

Buchanan, B., & Lappin, J. (1990). Restoring the soul of the family. *The Family Therapy Networker, 14*(6), 46–52.

Butler, R. N. (1963). The life review: An interpretation of reminiscence in the aged. *Psychiatry, 26,* 65–76.

Callahan, D. (1987). *Setting Limits.* New York: Simon and Schuster.

Canetto, S. S., Feldman, L. B., & Lupei, R. L. (1989). Suicidal persons and their partners: Individual and interpersonal dynamics. *Suicide and Life-Threatening Behavior, 19,* 237–248.

Caplan, G. (1964). *Principles of preventive psychiatry.* New York: Basic Books.

Caruth, E. G. (1991). Bruno Bettelheim's death: Further considerations. *The Psychologist Psychoanalyst, 11*(1), 6–7.

Clarke, J. J. (1981). Exploration of countertransference toward the dying. *American Journal of Orthopsychiatry, 51*(1), 71–77.

Coleman, J., & Errera, P. (1963). The general hospital emergency room and its psychiatric problems. *American Journal of Public Health, 53,* 1294–1301.

Coleman, M., & Zwerling, I. (1959). Psychiatric emergency clinic: A flexible way of meeting community mental health needs. *American Journal of Psychiatry, 115,* 980–984.

Comstock, B. S., & McDermott, M. (1975). Group therapy for patients who attempt suicide. *International Journal of Group Psychotherapy, 25,* 44–49.

Conroy, D. L. (1990). *Out of the nightmare. Recovery from depression and suicidal pain.* New York: New Library Press.

Conwell, Y. (1991). A failed suicide. Presented at the 24th Annual Conference of the American Association of Suicidology, April 19, 1991, Boston, MA.

Cooper, D. E. (1984). Group psychotherapy with the elderly: Dealing with loss and death. *American Journal of Psychotherapy, 38*(2), 203–214.

Costa, P. T., & McCrae, R. R. (1990). Personality disorders and the five factor model of personality. *Journal of Personality Disorder, 4,* 362–371.

de Shazer, S. (1988). *Clues: Investigating solutions in brief therapy.* New York: Norton.

De Vos, G. A. (1968). Suicide in cross-cultural perspective. In H. L. P. Resnik (Ed.), *Suicidal behaviors: Diagnosis and management.* Boston: Little, Brown & Co.

Domino, G. (1991). Attitudes of high school students toward suicide. In A. Leenaars, & S. Wenckstern (Eds.), *Suicide prevention in schools.* New York: Hemisphere Publishing Corporation.

Dumont, M. P. (March 1991). A gedanken experiment, part I: A bridge to nowhere. *Readings: A Journal of Reviews and Commentary in Mental Health,* 4–7.

Durkheim, E. (1951). *Suicide.* (J. A. Spaulding & G. Simpson, trans.). New York: The Free Press.

Ellis, W. D. (Ed.) (1938). *A source book in Gestalt psychology.* London: Routledge & Kegan Paul Ltd.

English, H. D., & English, A. C. (1958). *A comprehensive dictionary of psychological and psychoanalytic terms.* New York: Longmans, Green.

Erikson, E. (1950). *Childhood and society.* New York: Norton.

Estes, C. L., & Binney, E. A. (1989). The biomedicalization of aging: Dangers and dilemmas. *The Gerontologist, 29,* 587–596.

Fadiman, A. (1986). The liberation of Lolly and Gronky. *Life,* December, 1986, 71–94.

Farberow, N. L., Shneidman, E. S., & Leonard, C. V. (1965). Suicide among schizophrenic hospital patients. In E. S. Shneidman & N. L. Farberow (Eds.), *The cry for help.* New York: McGraw-Hill, 78–109. Reprinted in Shneidman, E. S., Barberow, N. L. & Litman, R. E. (Eds.). *The psychology of suicide.* New York: Science House.

Farberow, N. L. (1967). Crisis, disaster and suicide: Theory and therapy. In E. S. Sheidman (Ed.), *Essay in self-destruction.* New York: Science House.

Farberow, N. L. (1968). Group psychotherapy with suicidal persons. In H. L. P. Resnik, (Ed.). *Suicidal behaviors: Diagnosis and management.* Boston: Little, Brown & Co., 328–340.

Farberow, N. L. (1972). Vital process in suicide prevention: Group psychotherapy as a community of concern. *Life-Threatening Behavior, 2,* 239–251.

Feiner, A. H., & Epstein, L. (Eds.). (1979). *Countertransference: The therapist's contribution to therapy.* New York: Jason Aronson.

Ferguson, J. H. (1991). Charge to the panel. Presented at the Consensus Development Conference on the Diagnosis and Treatment of Depression in Late Life. November 4–6, 1991, Bethesda, MD.

Fiedler, F. E. (1950). The concept of an ideal therapeutic relationship. *Journal of Consulting Psychology, 14,* 239–245.

Fisher, J. (Spring 1973). Competence, effectiveness, intellectual functioning, and aging. *The Gerontologist, 13,* 61–68.

Fowers, B. J. (1990). Assessing dyadic patterns with standard marital interventions. *The Family Psychologist, 6*(3), 27–28.

Frank, J. (1973). *Persuasion and healing.* Baltimore: Johns Hopkins.

Freud, S. (1955). Group psychology and the analysis of the ego. In *Standard Edition (18,* 67–143). London: Hogarth Press. (Original work published 1921.)

Freud, S. (1957a). Five lectures on psychoanalysis. In *Standard edition (11,* 3–56). London: Hogarth Press. (Original work published 1910.)

Freud, S. (1957b). Mourning and melancholia. In *Standard edition (14,* 243–258). London: Hogarth Press. (Original work published 1917).

Freud, S. (1958). Recommendations for physicians practising psycho-analysis. In *Standard Edition (XII,* 109–120). London: Hogarth Press. (Original work published 1911.)

Furst, S, & Ostow, M. (1965). The psychodynamics of suicide. *Bulletin of the Academy of Medicine, Second Series, 42,* 190–204.

Gabriel, T. (Dec. 8, 1991). A fight to the death. *The New York Times Magazine,* 46–47, 84–88.

Gitelson, M. (1975). The emotional problems of elderly people. In W. C. Sze, (Ed.), *Human life cycle.* New York: Jason Aronson, 575–587.

Goldstein, K. (1939). *The organism. A holistic approach to biology derived from pathological data in man.* New York: American Book Company.

Gore, A., Jr. (1990). The homeless and the new homelessness in historical perspective. *American Psychologist, 45*(8), 960–962.

Gurian, B. S. (1986). The myth of the aged as asexual: Countertransference issues in therapy. *Hospital and Community Psychiatry, 37*(4), 345–346.

Gut, E. (1989). *Productive and unproductive depression.* New York: Basic Books.

Hackel, J. K., & Asimos, C. T. (1981). Resistances encountered in starting a group therapy program for suicide attempters in varied administrative settings. *Suicide and Life-Threatening Behavior, 11,* 93–98.

Haggerty, J. (1973). Suicidal behavior in a 70-year-old man: A case report. *Journal of Geriatric Psychiatry, 6,* 43–51.

Hawthorne, N. (1950). *The house of seven gables.* New York: Dodd-Mead.

Heiman, P. (1950). On countertransference. *International Journal of Psychoanalysis, 31,* 31–83.

Heller, J. (1979). *Good as gold.* New York: Simon & Schuster.

Hendin, H. (1969). *Black suicide.* New York: Basic Books.

Hendin, H. (1991). Psychodynamics of suicide, with particular reference to the young. *American Journal of Psychiatry, 148,* 1150–1158.

Hendrickson, R. (1990). *American literary anecdotes.* New York: Facts on File, 121.

Henisz, J. E., & Johnson, D. (1977). A crisis model revisited. *Comprehensive Psychiatry, 18*(2), 169.

Henry, A. F., & Short, J. F. (1954). *Suicide and homicide.* New York: Free Press.

Hooley, J. M. (1986). Expressed emotion and depression: Interactions between patients and high versus low EE spouses. *Journal of Abnormal Psychology, 95,* 237–246.

Horewitz, J. D. (1979). *Family Therapy and Transactional Analysis.* New York: Jason Aronson.

Humphry, D. (1991). *Final exit.* Eugene, OR: The Hemlock Society.

Indin, B. M. (1966). The crisis club: A group experience for suicidal patients. *Mental Hygiene, 50,* 280–290.

Jackson, D. D. (1965). Family rules: The marital *quid pro quo. Archives of General Psychiatry, 12,* 589–594.

Jacobs, J. (1971). *Adolescent suicide.* New York: Wiley–Interscience.

Kahana, R. J. (1979). Psychodynamic psychotherapy with the aged. *Journal of Geriatric Psychiatry, 12,* 71–100.

Kane, R. A. (1989). The biomedical blues. *The Gerontologist, 29,* 583–584.

Kaplan, K. J., and Maldavar, M. (1990). Suicide in the family. *Proceedings, 23rd Annual Meeting of the American Association of Suicidology.* New Orleans, LA. April 25–29, 1990. Denver, CO: American Association of Suicidology.

Karasu, B. T., & Richman, J. (1972). Marathon crisis intervention. *Proceedings, 80th Annual Convention, American Psychological Association,* 363–364.

Kastenbaum, R., & Ross, B. (1975). Historical perspectives on care. In J. G. Howells (Ed.), *Modern perspectives in the psychiatry of old age.* (421–449). New York: Brunner/Mazel.

Klein, M. (1975). A contribution to the psychogenesis of manic-depressive states. *In Love guilt and reparation & other works,* 1921–1945 (262–289). New York: Delacorte Press Seymour Lawrence. (Original work published 1935).

Klerman, G. L., Weissman, M. M., Rounsaville, B. J., & Chevron, E. S. (1984). *Interpersonal psychotherapy of depression.* New York: Basic Books.

Klopfer, W. G. (1984). The use of the Rorschach in brief clinical evaluation. *Journal of Personality Assessment, 48,* 654–659.

Kris, E. (1952). *Psychoanalytic explorations in art.* New York: International Universities Press.

Langsley, D. G., Kaplan, D. M., et al, (1968). *The treatment of families in crisis.* New York: Grune and Stratton.

Leenaars, A. A., Maris, R., McIntosh, J. L., & Richman, J., (Eds.). (1992). *Suicide and the older adult: A special issue of Suicide and Life-Threatening Behavior.* New York: Guilford Press.

Lesnoff-Caravaglia, G. (1987). Suicide in old age: Causes, clues, and concerns. In G. Lesnoff-Caravaglia (Ed.), *Handbook of applied genontology* (258–296). New York: Human Sciences Press.

Lester, D. (1987). The stability of national suicide rates in Europe. *Sociology and Social Research, 71,* 208.

Levinson, D. J., et al. (1978). *Seasons of a man's life.* New York: Knopf.

Lindemann, E. (1944). Symptomatology and management of acute grief. *American Journal of Psychiatry, 101,* 141–148.

Litman, R. E., & Tabachnick, N. D. (1968). Psychoanalytic therories of suicide. In H. L. P. Resnik (Ed.). *Suicidal behaviors: Diagnosis and management* (73–81). Boston: Little, Brown & Co.

Luborsky, L. (1984). *Principles of psychoanalytic psychotherapy: A manual for supportive-expressive treatment.* New York: Basic Books.

MacLennan, B. W., Saul, S., & Weiner, M. B. (Eds.). (1988). *Group psychotherapies for the elderly.* Madison, CT: American Group Psychotherapy Association Monograph 5/International Universities Press.

Mahler, M. S. (1968). *On human symbiosis and the vicissitudes of individuation. Vol. I: Infantile psychosis.* New York: International Universities Press.

Mahler, M. S., Pine, F., & Bergman, A. (1975). *The psychological birth of the human infant.* New York: Basic Books.

Maltsberger, J. T. (1986). *Suicide risks: The formulation of clinical judgement.* New York: New York University Press.

Maltsberger, J. T. (1991). Psychotherapy with older suicidal patients. *Journal of Geriatric Psychiatry, 24,* 217–234.

Maltsberger, J. T., & Buie, D. H. (1974). Countertransference hate in the treatment of suicidal patients. *Archives of General Psychiatry, 30,* 625–633.

Marks, M. (1985). Professional narcissism in psychotherapy. *Current Issues in Psychoanalytic Practice, 2,* 95–109.

Marshall, J. R. (1978). Changes in aged white male suicide: 1948–1972. *Journal of Gerontology, 33,* 763–768.

McCourtney, J. L. (1961). Suicide as a complication in group psychotherapy. *Military Medicine, 126,* 895–898.

McCulloch, G. (1990). The relationship of intergenerational reciprocity of aid to the morale of older parents: Equity and exchange theory comparisons. *Journal of Gerontology: Social Sciences, 45*(4), 150–155.

McIntosh, J. L., & Santos, J. F. (1985–86). Methods of suicide by age: Sex and race differences among the young and old. *International Journal of Aging and Human Development, 22,* 123–139.

McIntosh, J. L. (1991). U. S. Suicide: 1988 Official Final Data. Presented at the 23rd Annual Conference of the American Association of Suicidology, Boston, MA, April 1991.

McIntosh, J. L. (1992). Epidemiology in the elderly. In A. L. Leenaars, R. Maris, J. L. McIntosh, & J. Richman, (Eds.) *Suicide and the older adult.* New York: Guilford Press.

McMordie, W. R., & Blom, S. (1979). Life review therapy: Psychotherapy for the elderly. *Perspectives in Psychiatric Care, 4,* 162–166.

Medley, M. L. (1976). Satisfaction with life among persons sixty-five years and older: A causal model. *Journal of Gerontology, 31*(4), 448–455.

Meissner, W. W. (1978). *The paranoid process.* New York: Jason Aronson.

Middlebrook, D. W. (1991). *Anne Sexton: A biography.* Boston: Houghton-Mifflin.

Miller, R. E., & Shaskan, D. A. (1963). A note on the group management of a disgruntled suicidal patient. *International Journal of Group Psychotherapy, 13,* 216–218.

Minuchin, S. (1974). *Families and family therapy.* Cambridge, MA: Harvard University Press.

Moore, B. E., & Fine, B. D. (1990). *Psychoanalytic terms & concepts.* New Haven: Yale University Press.

Moss, L. M., & Hamilton, D. M. (1957). Psychotherapy of the suicidal patient. In

E. S. Shneidman & N. L. Farberow (Eds.), *Clues to suicide*. New York: McGraw-Hill.

Murphy, G. E., & Wetzel, R. D. (1990). The lifetime risk of suicide in alcoholism. *Archives of General Psychiatry, 47*, 383–392.

Naegele, K. D. (1965). Youth and society: Some observations. In E. E. Erikson (Ed.), *The challenge of youth* (51–75). Garden City, New York: Anchor Books.

Nathan, G. J. (1942). Aesthetic jurisprudence. In W. Burnett (Ed.), *This is my best* (727–737). New York: Dial (Original work published 1922).

Neill, J. R., & Knisker, D. P. (Eds.). (1982). *From psyche to system: The evolving therapy of Carl Whitaker*. New York: Guilford Press.

Osgood, N. J., & McIntosh, J. L. (1986). *Suicide and the elderly: An annotated bibliography and review*. Westport, CT: Greenwood Press.

Payne, E. S. (1975). Depression and suicide. In J. G. Howells (Ed.), *Modern perspectives in the psychiatry of old age* (290–312). New York: Brunner/Mazel.

Peck, R. (1975). Psychological developments in the second half of life. In W. C. Sze (Ed.), *Human life cycle* (609–625). New York: Jason Aronson.

Pennebaker, J. W. (1990). *Opening up: The healing power of confiding in others*. New York: Morrow.

Pittman, F. S. (1987). *Turning points. Treating families in transition and crisis*. New York: Norton.

Portwood, D. (1978). *Common sense suicide*. New York: Dodd-Mead.

Pronsati, M. P. (August 6, 1990). Know signs of depression, OTs told. *Advance for Occupational Therapists, 7*.

Reichelt, S., & Christiensen, B. (1990). Reflections during a study on family therapy with drug addicts. *Family Process, 29*, 273–287.

Reines, A. J. (1991). The morality of suicide: A surresponse. *Journal of Reform Judaism, 39*, 73–80.

Reiss, D. (1968). The suicide six: Observations on suicidal behavior and group function. *International Journal of Social Psychiatry, 14*, 201–212.

Resnick, H. L. P., & Cantor, J. M. (1970). Suicide and aging. *Journal of the American Geriatrics Society, 18*, 152–158.

Richman, J. (1967). Reporting diagnostic test results to patients and their families. *Journal of Projective Techniques and Personality Assessment, 31*, 62–70.

Richman, J. (1971). Family determinants of suicidal potential. In D. B. Anderson & L. J. McClean (Eds.), *Identifying suicide potential*. New York: Behavioral Publications.

Richman, J. (1975). Precipitants and motives of attempted suicide in younger and older subjects. Presented at the Fifth Conference of the International Gerontological Association, Jerusalem, Israel.

Richman, J. (1979a). Mass suicide as a family affair: The Peoples' Temple in Guyana. Presented at the 12th Annual Conference of the American Association of Suicidology, April 21, 1979. Denver, CO.

Richman, J. (1979b). A couples therapy group on a geriatric service. *Journal of Geriatric Psychiatry, 12*, 203–213.

Richman, J. (1981). Marital psychotherapy and terminal illness. In A. S. Gurman (Ed.) *Questions and answers in the practice of family therapy*. New York: Brunner/Mazel.

Richman, J. (1984). The family therapy of suicidal adolescents: Promises and pitfalls. In H. S. Sudak, A. B. Ford, & N. B. Ruchforth (Eds.), *Suicide in the young* (393–406). Boston: John Wrights, PSG Inc.

Richman, J. (1986). *Family therapy for suicidal people.* New York: Springer Publishing Co.

Richman, J. (1990). Suicide pácts and media bias. Presented at the 98th Annual Conference on the American Psychological Association, Boston, MA, August 1990.

Richman, J. (1991). Suicide and the elderly. In A. A. Leenaars (Ed.), *Life span perspectives of suicide* (153–167). New York: Plenum Press.

Richman, J., & Davidoff, I. (1971). Interaction testing and counseling as a form of crisis intervention during marital therapy. *Proceedings, 79th Annual Convention, American Psychological Association, 6,* 439–440.

Richman, J., & Kahn, L. (1986). Attitudes of physicians to physicians suicide. Presented at the bi-annual conference of the International Association For Suicide Prevention, September 1–4, 1986, Vienna, Austria.

Richman, J., & Eyman, J. R. (1990). Psychotherapy of suicide: Individual, group, and family approaches. In D. Lester (Ed.) *Current concepts of suicide* (139–158). Philadelphia, PA: The Charles Press.

Richman, J., Brooks, A., Carter, B. F., and Ross, C. (1991). Group suicide pre- and post-vention, across the ages. Presented at the 24th Annual Conference of the American Association of Suicidology, April 20, 1991, Boston, MA.

Richman, L. (1969). Sensory training in the treatment of geriatric patients. *American Journal of Occupational Therapy, 23,* 254–257.

Roberts, M. C. (1985). A plea for professional civility. *Professional Psychology: Research and Practice, 16,* 474.

Rogers, C. (1942). *Counseling and psychotherapy.* Boston: Houghton-Mifflin.

Rogers, C. (1951). *Client-centered therapy.* Boston: Houghton-Mifflin.

Rosen, J. N. (1970). Some reflections on the problem. In A. W. R. Sipe (Ed.), *Hope: Psychiatry's Commitment.* New York: Brunner/Mazel.

Ross. E. P., & Motto, J. A. (1984). Group counseling for suicidal adolescents. In H. S. Sudak, A. G. Ford, & M. B. Rushforth (Eds.), *Suicide in the young.* Boston: John Wright, PSG Publishing.

Rossi, P. H. (1990). The old and the new homelessness in historical perspective. *American Psychologist, 45*(8), 954–959.

Roth, P. (1991). *Patrimony: A true story.* New York: Simon & Schuster.

Rubenstein, A. (1973). *My young years.* New York: Alfred A. Knopf.

Rutz, W., Walinder, J., Eberhard G., Holmberg, G., von Knorring, A.-L., von Knorring, L., Wisted, B., & Aberg-Wisted, A. (1989). An educational program on depressive disorders for general practitioners on Gotland: background and evaluation. *Acta Psychiatrica Scandinavia, 79,* 19–26.

Ryff, C. D. (1989). In the eye of the beholder: Views of psychological well-being among middle-aged and older adults. *Psychology and Aging, 4,* 195–210.

Sabbath, J. C. (1969). The expendable child. *Journal of the American Academy of Child Psychiatry, 8,* 272–289.

Sanborn, D. E., Niswander, G. D., & Casey, T. M. (1970). The family physician and suicide prevention. *American Family Physician/GP, 1,* 75–78.

Sandler, A. M. (1982). Psychoanalysis and psychoanalytic psychotherapy of the older patient. A developmental crisis in an aging patient: Comments on development and adaptation. *Journal of Geriatric Psychiatry, 15*(1), 11–32.

Schuckman, T. (1975). *Aging is not for sissies.* Philadelphia: The Westminster Press.

Schur, M. (1972). *Freud: Living and dying.* New York: International Universities Press.

Segal, H. (1958). Fear of death: Notes on the analysis of an old man. *International Journal of Psycho-Analysis, 39,* 178–181.

Selye, H. (1975). *Stress without distress.* New York: Signet.

Shea, M. T., Pilkonis, P. A., Beckham, E., Collins, J. R., et al. (1990). Personality disorders and treatment outcome in the NIMH Treatment of Depression Collaborative Research Program. *American Journal of Psychiatry, 146,* 711–718.

Sher, T. G., Baucom, D. H., & Larus, J. M. (1990). Communication patterns and response to treatment among depressed and nondepressed maritally distressed couples. *Journal of Family Psychology, 4*(1), 63–79.

Shneidman, E. S. (1985). *Definition of suicide.* New York: Wiley.

Shneidman, E. S. (1988). Some reflections of a founder. *Suicide and Life-Threatening Behavior, 18,* 1–12.

Shneidman, E. S., Farberow, N. L., & Leonard, C. V. (1970). Suicidal risk among schizophrenic patients. In E. S. Shneidman, N. L. Farberow, & R. E. Litman, (Eds.), *The psychology of suicide* (307–324). New York: Science House.

Silove, D., Parker, G., & Manicavasagar, V. (1990). Perceptions of general and specific therapist behaviors. *Journal of Nervous & Mental Disease, 178*(5), 292–299.

Slakter, E. (1987). *Countertransference.* Northvale, NJ: Jason Aronson.

Smith, K., & Eyman, J. (1988). Ego structure and object differentiation in suicidal patients. In H. Lerner & P. Lerner (Eds.), *Primitive mental states and the Rorschach* (175–202). Madison, CT: International Universities Press.

Steiner, J. F. (1967). *Treblinka.* New York: Simon & Schuster.

Stewart, J. T. (1991). Diagnosing and treating depression in the hospitalized elderly. *Geriatrics, 46,* 64–72.

Stone, W. N. (1991). Treatment of the chronically mentally ill: An opportunity for the group therapist. *International Journal of Group Psychotherapy, 41,* 11–22.

Strickler, M., & Allgeyer, J. (1967). The crisis group: A new application of crisis theory. *Social Work, 12,* 28–32.

Styron, W. (1990). *Darkness visible.* New York: Random House.

Strean, H. S. (1991). Colluding illusions among analytic candidates, their supervisors, and their patients: A major factor in some treatment impasses. *Psychoanalytic Psychology, 8,* 403–414.

Swados, E. (1991). *The four of us.* New York: Farrar, Straus & Giroux.

Szasz, T. (1986). The case against suicide prevention. *The American Psychologist, 41,* 806–812.

Tabachnick, N. D. (1961). Interpersonal relations in suicidal attempts. *Archives of General Psychiatry, 4,* 42–47.

Targum, S. D. (1988). Genetic issues in treatment. In J. F. Clarkin, G. L. Haas, and I. R. Glick (Eds.), *Affective disorders and the family* (196–212). New York: Guilford.

Toolan, J. M. (1984). Suicide and suicide attempts in children and adolescents. In H. S. Sudak, A. G. Ford, & N. B. Rushforth (Eds.) *Suicide in the young.* Boston: John Wright, PSG Publishing.

Tross, S., & Blum, J. E. (1988). A review of group therapy with the older adult: Practice and research. In B. W. MacLennan, S. Saul, & M. B. Weiner (Eds.), *Group psychotherapies for the elderly*(3–29). Madison, CT: American Group Psychotherapy Association Monograph 5/International Universities Press.

Truax, C. G., & Carkhuf, R. R. (1967). *Toward effective counseling and psychotherapy: Training and practice.* Chicago: Aldine.

Veatch, R. M. (1976). *Death, dying, and the biological revolution.* New Haven, CT: Yale University Press.

Vollhardt, L. T. (1991). Psychoneuroimmunology: A literature review. *American Journal of Orthopsychiatry, 61*(1), 35–47.

Watts, C. A. H. (1961). The problem of suicide in general practice. *Proceedings of the Royal Society of Medicine, 54,* 10–11.

Watzlawick, P., Beavin, J. H., & Jackson, D. (1967). *Pragmatics of human communication.* New York: Norton.

Wickett, A. (1989). *Double exit.* Eugene, OR: The Hemlock Society.

Weinstein, C. (1990). "The question of medical psychotherapy": Comment. *American Journal of Psychotherapy, 44*(2), 312–313.

Weiss, J., Sampson, H., and the Mount Zion Psychotherapy Research Group (1986). *The psychoanalytic process: Theory, clinical observations, and empirical research.* New York: Guilford.

Wells, C. F., & Rabiner, E. L. (1973). The conjoint family diagnostic interview and the family index of tension. *Family Process, 12,* 127–144.

White, E. B. (1959). The morning of the day they did it. In A. Boucher (Ed.), A treasury of great science fiction, *Volume Two* (322–333).

Wiesel, E. (1990). Treasured family is the secret wealth of 'The Rothschilds.' *The New York Times Entertainment Section,* September 23, 1990, 5–6.

Winnicott, D. W. (1965). *The maturational processes and the facilitating environment.* New York: International Universities Press.

The Wolf-Man. (1971). *The Wolf-Man.* New York: Basic Books.

Wolinsky, M. A. (1990). *A heart of wisdom.* New York: Brunner/Mazel.

World Federation for Mental Health (1989). *The declaration of Luxor. Human rights for the mentally ill.* Adopted at the Annual Conference of the WFMH, January 17, 1989. Luxor, Egypt.

Zigler, E., & Glick, M. (1988). Is paranoid schizophrenia really camouflaged depression? *American Psychologist, 43,* 284–290.

Zimmerman, J. K., & LaSorsa, V. A. (1992). Being the family's therapist: An integrative approach. Presented at the 25th Annual Conference of the American Association of Suicidology, Chicago, IL, April 2, 1992.

Zuk, G. H. (1990). Conflict cycle in family therapy. *The Family Psychologist, 6*(3), 38, 45.

Index